# HUMAN RIGHTS:
# MEANING AND HISTORY

By

## Michael Palumbo

**AN ANVIL ORIGINAL**

*under the general editorship of*
LOUIS L. SNYDER

ROBERT E. KRIEGER PUBLISHING COMPANY
MALABAR, FLORIDA
1982

Original Edition    1982

Printed and Published by
**ROBERT E. KRIEGER PUBLISHING COMPANY, INC.**
**KRIEGER DRIVE**
**MALABAR, FLORIDA 32950**

Copyright © 1982 by
MICHAEL PALUMBO

Printed in the United States of America

**Library of Congress Cataloging in Publication Data**

Palumbo, Michael.
    Human rights, meaning and history.

    (An Anvil original)
    Summary: Surveys the philosophy and history of
human rights, as well as current human rights
problems, under various political systems in all
parts of the world.
    1. Civil rights—History.    2. Civil rights—
Addresses, essays, lectures. [1. Civil rights]
I. Title.
JC571.P25                    323.4'09              81-18592
ISBN 0-89874-259-5                                 AACR2

34, 573

# PREFACE

The term human rights was widely used in the period immediately after World War II and again during the administration of President Jimmy Carter. But the concept of human rights has a long history. The present volume is designed to trace the development of the concept from ancient to modern times. Obviously, in one brief volume it is not possible to give detailed consideration to every aspect of the subject. The central theme of the work is the evolution of the civil and political concepts of human rights in Western civilization. However, a purely ethnocentric approach has been avoided and as much as possible about human rights in the Third World has been included. There has also been an effort to consider the Marxist view which gives precedence to economic and social rights over civil and political rights. Indeed, the aim has been to give a survey of the philosophy, history, and current problems of human rights in various parts of the world and under divergent political systems.

The importance of considering human rights in the decades ahead cannot be doubted. Nowhere in the world are people completely secure in their civil, political, social, cultural, and economic rights. Even in those countries where certain rights have been attained, a constant struggle is necessary to avoid their erosion. In the United States, the declining standard of living, computerized surveillance, and the power of special interest groups all represent serious threats to individual rights. An understanding of the meaning and history of human rights is essential if our way of life is to flourish.

In composing this volume, I received considerable support and encouragement from many sources. Amnesty International was most generous in supplying much useful material. Helga Feder and the staff of the City University Graduate Center Library helped me locate many difficult-to-obtain sources. Yolanda Quitman gave me considerable information on the women's movement. A special thanks goes to Joel Agee with whom I had many stimulating conversations on human rights. For help in preparation of the manuscript, thanks go to Julia Klein and Betty Einerman.

New York City,                                    *Michael Palumbo*
Spring 1981.

# TABLE OF CONTENTS

PREFACE

## Part I — Human Rights: Meaning and History

## Part II — Readings

# Part I

HUMAN RIGHTS:  MEANING AND HISTORY

# 1

# THE MEANING OF HUMAN RIGHTS

**Definition of Human Rights.** Human rights can best be defined as those rights which human beings have simply because they are human beings. These rights are quite independent of social circumstance or the level of achievement which an individual has attained. A person's human rights can not be relinquished, transferred, or forfeited by the actions of another individual. Additional rights which a person may have are largely derived from the human rights which are basic to each individual. The notion of human rights is an ancient one, and in the Western tradition goes back at least to the *Old Testament.* In their development in the modern world, a landmark figure is the English philosopher John Locke (1632-1704). His basic theme was man's inherent right to life, liberty, and property, especially against the incursions of arbitrary government. Human rights have subsequently been thought to include due process of law, freedom from cruel and inhumane punishment, and freedom of religion. Other rights often mentioned are freedom of speech and press. According to the Declaration of Independence, "the pursuit of happiness" is an inalienable right. The French "Declaration of the Rights of Man and the Citizen" of 1789 *(see Reading No. 1)* has been one of the most influential formulations of human rights.

**Human Rights and Natural Law.** A common basis and justification for human rights has been the concept of natural law. Though it remains unwritten, natural law consists of a code which reasonable men presumably agree upon as the basis to govern all human actions. Natural law takes precedence over all man-made laws, rules, and customs. Most adherents of natural law believe that it is derived from a Supreme Being who governs the universe in an orderly fashion.

The medieval philosopher St. Thomas Aquinas (1225-1274) was one of the most noted exponents of a Divine derivation for natural law. In his *Summa Theologica* he wrote that natural law was communicated by God to man and discoverable by unaided human reason. Some, like the great Durch jurist Hugo Grotius (1585-1645), based the concept of natural law on reason pure and simple. Grotius stated that natural law was self-evident in the same sense that the truths of mathematics were held to be self-evident. The truths of mathematics would remain in force even if God could be conceived of as nonexistent.

Natural law consists of both obligations and rights. Simply stated, man's basic obligation under natural law is to do good and avoid evil. The idea that there are certain inalienable human rights above and beyond man-made legislation is accepted by most adherents of natural law. In cases where there have been massive violations of human rights without any apparent violation of national statutes, natural law has been invoked. This happened when the leading Nazi war criminals were put on trial at Nuremberg after World War II. In the absence of any specific law against military aggression and genocide, natural law was invoked in order to justify the prosecution of some of the Nazi leaders who had violated the human rights of millions of people. Although the natural law for the case had never been written down or codified, the crimes committed were said to have violated the accepted standard for civilized men.

**Critics of the Idea of Inherent Human Rights.** The theory of human rights derived from an unwritten natural law has not been without its critics. Notable among them was the German philosopher Georg W.F. Hegel (1770-1831). He believed that history was governed by the "Absolute," of which all its separate events were manifestations. In human life, the most important agent of history was the state, which Hegel saw as the creator and protector of values, including the human rights of individuals. Many of Hegel's followers argued that rights belonged not to individuals but to societies and communities. Karl Marx (1818-1883), who was greatly influenced by Hegel, regarded the classic concept of human rights derived from natural law as a "bourgeois" illusion. As a collectivist, he was hostile to the emphasis on individualism which the doctrine implied.

Jeremy Bentham (1748-1832), an influential British radical reformer, also objected to the concept of human rights derived from natural law. He believed that they were a poor substitute for real laws which could effectuate positive change in society. Bentham believed that governments which issued pious declarations of the rights of man were making statements which cost nothing, and which tended to delay much needed substantive reform. *(See Reading No. 2.)*

Many conservatives have been critical of the doctrine of inherent human rights. Some have denied that "man" existed in the abstract, apart from his station in life. As Joseph De Maistre (1754-1821) stated "I have seen in my time Frenchmen, Italians, Russians, etc. but as for *Man* I declare I never met him in my life; if he exists, it is without my knowledge." To conservatives such as De Maistre, tranquility in society depended on people accepting their particular status. They believed that hierarchy in society was a vital stabilizing factor, and that the concept of social equality for all was a most pernicious doctrine. Human inequality was of necessity so profound and indelible that it was cruel to pretend to the lower classes that they had an inalienable right to certain freedoms and powers that would always belong exclusively to the higher ranks.

**The Modern Concept of Human Rights.** Since 1945 there has been a renewed interest in the doctrine of human rights. The atrocities which took place during World War II convinced many people that human rights had to be established on a firm foundation, to prevent the recurrence of such horrors. During the war there were a number of declarations by Allied leaders that made it clear that human rights was one of their principal war aims. On January 1, 1942, all the Allied powers signed a "Declaration of the United Nations" in which it was stated that "complete victory over their enemies is essential to defend life, liberty, independence and religious freedom, and to preserve human rights and justice in their own lands as well as in other lands." In October 1942, Winston Churchill spoke of the time "when this world struggle ends with the enthronement of human rights."

In 1948, the United Nations adopted the Universal Declaration of Human Rights. *(See Reading No. 3.)* Much of this document is basically a continuation of the classic definitions of human rights, based on natural law. The rights of life, liberty, property, equality, justice, and pursuit of happiness are covered in the first twenty articles. But, in addition, the Declaration goes on to assert rights which substantially broaden the traditional concept. Article 22 asserts that everyone "has the right to social security." Subsequent articles proclaim the right to education, to equal pay for equal work, the right to an adequate standard of living, and the right to leisure, including "periodic holidays with pay."

It is a controversial point as to whether the inclusion of "economic and social rights" represent an improvement in the concept of human rights. Previous definitions of the concept had usually been limited to "political and civil rights." In the 1948 Declaration, "economic and social rights" were included at the insistence of the Communist-bloc nations. Their system negates the possibility of fulfilling the traditional human rights; but they could claim that they provide social security, education, and "periodic holidays with pay." For our purposes, we shall concentrate on the classic definition of human rights, but we will certainly not ignore the economic and social rights which ideally should be an addition to rather than a substitute for political and civil rights.

# 2

# HUMAN RIGHTS IN ANTIQUITY

**The Hebrews.** It is impossible to trace the beginning of human rights to any specific date or culture. However, in ancient times, the Hebrews were among the first to put into practice a policy of respect for the dignity of every individual. Judaism holds that God endowed all human beings with his image. In the *Bible,* man can speak to God an on occasion can even argue with him because it was for man's sake that the universe was created.

Judaism began as the tribal religion of the Hebrews which did not differ greatly from the beliefs of other primitive peoples. Eventually, it evolved from a cult pre-occupied with tribal warfare into a religion which taught justice and mercy. In place of burnt sacrifices the favor of the deity Yahweh was to be won by caring for widows and the fatherless and by kindness and charity. The prophets of Israel tore away the shackles of superstition from the free life of the spirit to make religion a guide for the common man in the trials and difficulties of everyday life. Yahweh's world was to be different from any other because it was to be a world at peace. Isaiah the prophet envisaged a time when the people of the earth "shall beat their swords into plowshares and their spears into pruning hooks; nation shall not lift up sword against nation nor shall they learn war any more."

Judaism taught that respect should be shown to non-Jews living among the children of Israel. In the book of Leviticus the Jews were told: You shall have one law for the stranger and citizen alike: for I the Lord am your God." The Hebrews were also much more respectful of women and slaves than other ancient peoples. Women, it was believed, shared the divine image. Their lives, limbs, and property were accorded the same respect accorded to those of men. In ancient Israel, women had definite prop-erty rights. What a woman acquired during her marriage by gift from friends or inheritance from relatives remained hers. A woman's physical person was protected. A husband had no right to kill or seriously injure his wife even if he found her in the commission of adultery. Rape was seriously punished. The *Old Testament* contains numerous examples of women who played a key role in Jewish tradition. Debra was a prophet of Israel. Other women, such as Judith, Esther, and Rebecca, greatly influenced important events in the history of the Hebrew people.

Judaism mandated a code for the treatment of domestic slaves who, in ancient Israel, more nearly resembled serfs or indentured servants. Under the law a slave was to enjoy the same food, clothing, and shelter as his master. If a slave was mistreated it was possible for him to gain his freedom. The law governing homicide recognized no difference if the victim was a non-Jewish slave or a Jewish freemen. The slave's wife and children were not sold with him, as was the custom in most other contemporaneous cultures. The master was obliged to support the slave's dependents. The slave could acquire property and redeem himself to freedom. At most, his bondage would last six years. Enslaved prisoners of war however were treated very harshly by the Hebrews.

**The Greeks.** Another people who contributed to our concept of human rights were the Greeks. In ancient times their mountainous land was divided into independent city-states most of which had a well-developed civic culture. The Greeks passionately debated the art of government and it was from them that we get such words as "democracy" and "tyranny." Most Greek city-states granted their citizens clearly defined civil rights such as *isogoria,* or equal freedom of speech, and *insonomia,* which implied equality before the law. In ancient Athens, the general assembly of all freemen, the *ecclesia,* was the sovereign body. After the reforms of Cleisthenes (6th century B.C.), army service and civil administration were opened more widely to the poorer classes. Pericles (490-429 B.C.), the greatest Athenian statesman, made democracy complete for all freemen. To ancient Greeks, however, the mere posession of rights was not enough. A good citizen used those rights for his own and for the common good.

Of course, Greek democracy did not constitute human rights in our modern sense. Women had very few rights in ancient Athens. Slavery was widespread. Indeed, there probably were more slaves than freemen in most Greek city-states. But compared to other contemporary civilizations, the ancient Greeks were remarkably advanced in their sense of human values and the dignity which they attributed to the common man.

This is particularly noticeable in Greek philosophy. Aristotle (384-322 B.C.) considered the role which justice should play in human affairs. He believed that honors and riches in society should be granted on the basis of the efforts expended or the qualities which were displayed by each individual. Aristotle did not believe in a system in which hereditary class status should determine social rank. Like Socrates and Plato he was concerned about ethics and the creation of the ideal society.

The ancient Greeks were the first to develop the concept of natural law. This can clearly be seen in the play *Antigone,* written by Sophocles (469-406 B.C.) in the fifth century B.C. In this work the author suggests that there is an unwritten natural law which takes precedence over all man-made legislation. The King, Creon, orders that Polynices his enemy who had been killed in battle should be left unburied. Antigone, the sister of Polynices, believes that the King is violating the right to burial which she believes belongs to every man. The play revolves around the conflict between established authority as exemplified by the King and the "immutable unwritten laws of heaven" which Antigone attempts to uphold.

The school of Greek philosophy called Stoicism accepted the idea of nautral law. The Stoics believed that justice is the natural expression of the law of reason ordained by God. They spoke of "one world" animated by a rational principle drawing all men together in brotherhood. They denied any difference between Greeks and

foreigners (who were usually referred to as barbarians).
They also saw no difference between freemen and slaves.
Unfortunately, however, the Stoics kept their philosophy
aloof from politics. Thus, they raised no voice against
slavery as an institution.

**Rome**.    Like most of the Mediterranean world,
Greece was eventually conquered by the Romans. Although they were primarily warriors and conquerors, the
Romans did make contribution to the advancement of
civilization particularly in their dissemination of Greek
culture. They were also great lawgivers in their own
right. The Roman Twelve Tables, which date from 449
B.C., placed emphasis on the necessity for a proper trial,
the presentation of evidence and proof, and the illegality
of bribery in judicial proceedings. All these are concepts
of law which have survived to our own day. The chief
contribution of the Romans to the advancement of freedom was in the extension of Roman citizenship from the
tribes in and around the early city of Rome to the whole
of Italy and eventually to all their imperial conquests.
The Romans did not attempt to exterminate other peoples or enslave them unless they revolted against or resisted imperial rule. The gradual extension of Roman citizenship reflected an acceptance of the people that were
conquered.

In ruling their Empire, the Romans did not attempt
to impose their own law but developed *jus gentium,* or
the law of peoples. This, it was believed, was the minimum of universal law which was found to be the same
everywhere. *Jus gentium* was regarded as a law common
to all mankind based on the nature of things and the general sense of equity obtaining among all men. It was a
sort of natural law exacting recognition everywhere
because of its inherent reasonableness. Most of *jus gentium*
came from Roman law but it was that portion of Roman
law which was fundamentally in accordance with the
private law of other nations. *Jus gentium* was greatly

appreciated by the conquered people who lived under Roman rule. It became a shield and a protector against the arbitrary power of Roman governors or the unlawful acts of fellow citizens. Its use was an important step in the development of human rights.

**Cicero.** The Greek philosophy of Stocism gained many converts in ancient Rome. Among those who studied it were the Emperors Marcus Aurelius (121-180 A.D.) and Justinian (502-565 A.D.). The great Roman jurist and statesman Marcus Tullius Cicero (106-43 B.C.) was influenced by it. He proposed a well-developed conception of natural law *(jus naturale),* which was eternal and immutable and which applied to all people at all times. God, he believed, was the source of this law. According to Cicero, natural law bound all men in such a way that "whoever is disobedient is fleeing from himself and denying his human nature." In his writings, Cicero recognized the essential equality of all men. *(See Reading No. 4.)*

**Christianity.** To a large extent the moral philosophy of Judaism was spread over the Mediterranean world through Christianity. The great difference between the teachings of Jesus and Judaism was the Christain claim to universality. From a very early stage the new religion was disseminated among all peoples and was not identified as the faith of any one tribe or nation. There are no "chosen people" in Christiantiy. Greeks, Romans, as well as Hebrews, were converted by the disciples of Chirst.

Another aspect of Christianity which supports human rights is the concept of the immortality of the soul. This doctrine lays emphasis on each man's importance and worth as an individual. Every human being was created by God and is destined for eternal life. This being the case, each person has the right to be treated with respect because he is more than a cog in a wheel but a special and unique creation of God. Chirstianity places importance on the salvation of the individual rather than the redemption of any particular people or nation.

In the teaching of Jesus, if not in modern Christianity, there was a turning away from ceremony in favor of upright living. In most other religions and even in early Judaism, ritual was so much a thing apart that only the priests knew how to conduct it. But to Jesus as to some of the later Hebrew prophets, sacerdotalism, instead of being the heart of religion, tended to become an impediment to its full realization. Previously holiness had been a negative rather than a positive concept emphasizing the separation of divinity from normal things. Jesus taught, however, that each man can attain holiness by a perfection of the inner life and just dealing with his fellow man. In the *New Testament* we see that Jesus denounced the "scribes and Pharisees" who treated the "law of Moses" almost like magic formulae, the rigid observance of which would bring automatic sanctity. To Jesus mere compliance with ritual was not the road to salvation.

Associated with Chirstianity is a social philosophy which upholds the dignity of the individual, particularly the poor and oppressed of the world. This is typified by the Sermon on the Mount. *(See Reading No. 5.)* Jesus taught that the disinherited of the earth would find in the world to come a "house with many mansions" prepared and held in readiness for them by the loving Father of all mankind. This was a more definite and humanly appealing message to the poor than the promise of any other religion. St. Paul stated that of the great trilogy, faith, hope, and charity, "the greatest of these is charity." Therefore, in Christianity the best preparation for the life to come is to love one's neighbor as well as to love God. Many of the Fathers of the Church appreciated the conception of Christianity as a religion of social service. Gregory Nazianzen stated "the service of Jesus is perfect freedom."

**Islam**.    Our indebtedness to the Judeo-Christian tradition as well as to Greco-Roman civilization does not justify the ethnocentric view that human rights is a purely Western phenomenon. Other cultures, traditions, and religions have developed ideas which are highly supportive of human rights. Islam, which is practiced by hundreds of millions of people in Africa, the Middle East, and Asia, has many provisions which promote the dignity of the individual. Founded by Mohammed (570-632), Islam borrowed from Christianity the idea of the immortality of the soul. All people are seen as equal children of Adam. Moslems have always shown a noticeable tolerance for nonbelievers under their control. Non-Moslem communities were generally permitted to judge themselves and administer their own local affairs. At the court of the Sultan, Jewish and Christian scholars and scientists always held an honored place. Indeed, much of the machinery of bureaucracy in Moslem countries was for many centuries in the hands of nonbelievers.

Islam is an intensely personal religion. It has no priesthood to serve as intermediary between man and God for the imams are prayer-leaders rather than a clergy in the Christian sense. Five times a day the Moslem true believer prays. All participate in these periodic prayer sessions which constitute a form of spiritual democracy. In Islam all are subject to the will of Allah. The life of even the greatest prince or saintliest holy man is governed by the will of God.

In comparison to pre-Islamic Arab religion, Mohammed's teachings represent a definite advance in its attitude toward the poor, orphans, and women. Although slavery was retained, slaves gained legal rights, especially the right to buy freedom with their earned wages. Emancipation of slaves, although not required, was encouraged as an act of religious merit. Female infanticide, previously widely practiced, was forbidden. Personal revenge for murder or other criminal acts was restricted. Justice was meted out by religious leaders strictly according to the rules of the *Koran.* Divorce laws were spelled out in the *Koran,* with provisions for the children of dissolved marriages.

**Confucianism.** The teaching of Confucius (551-479 B.C.) has been one of the greatest influences on Chinese life for almost 2500 years. The basic aim of the philosophy

of Confucius—the product of an era of feudalism and un-
settled conditions—was to secure an ordered society by
the exercise of the most deeply rooted instincts, those
rooted in family relations. Confucius stressed the importance of showing respect to one's family including one's
long-departed ancestors. But he also taught respect for
all mankind, which he saw as one large family. Confucian
teaching is comprised of a set of morals based upon the
fundamental principle of man's inherent goodness. This
sense of a universal human society based upon mankind's
innate goodness gave strong support to ideals of peace
between rulers as well as within their states.

Confucius was greatly concerned about the problem
of good government. He stressed the primacy of morals
over law, particularly unjust law. Although he preached
reverence for authority, this loyalty was always to be
tempered by moral judgment and the ethical man did not
owe allegiance to a tyrannical government. Confucius himself went into exile several times in various parts of China
rather than serve a ruler who violated the rights of his subjects. For Confucius, the ideal society would be that in
which the innate goodness of mankind could have a
chance to show itself under a ruler seeking the same end
as his people.

A central tenet of Confucianism is the Golden Rule.
It stated: "Do not do to others what you do not like
when done to yourself." This rule demonstrates a concern
for morality and a respect for every individual and his
place in society. Confucius also stressed the importance
of harmony and equilibrium in human affairs. This is
reflected in the importance which the Chinese place on
self-control. If one keeps his self-control, he is more likely
to respect the rights of his neighbor and maintain peace in
society.

**Buddhism.** The founder of Buddhism, Siddhartha
Gautama (563–483 B.C.), was born in what is now Nepal.
His teachings eventually spread to China, Japan, and
southeast Asia, and for some time, India. Siddhartha

Gautama lived the early part of his life as a prince. At about the age of thirty he left home to become an ascetic. Eventually, he became the Buddha, or the "Enlightened One." What he had come to see was not a doctrine for initiates only but truths which could be grasped by anyone. Buddhism preached man's respect for his fellow man. The Buddha stated: "Whoever would care for me should care for the sick." Buddhism stresses caring for the needs of the underprivileged as a great good. Buddhism emphasizes love as an important part of human relations even with one's enemies. An ancient Buddhist scripture states: "For hatred does not even cease by hatred; hatred ceases by love." Buddhism promotes the concept of ethical discipline. From this commitment come some of the earliest and most enduring affirmations of human rights. A follower of right action and right livelihood must refrain from all sorts of ignoble occupations such as trading in arms, in living beings, in intoxicants, in poison, or from taking a life or stealing.

Buddhism was a serious challenge to the solidifying notions of caste and untouchability in India. It recognized no distinctions among men and it has a democratic structure. Even the preceptors of monastaries have to be selected by the consensus of all the monks. Converts are encouraged only if they themselves come to the conclusion that truth and reason verify the Buddha's teachings. The decision is left up to each individual.

# 3

# THE DEVELOPMENT OF CIVIL LIBERTIES
## IN GREAT BRITAIN

**Human Rights in the Middle Ages.** After the fall of
the Roman Empire, Europe entered the Middle Ages.
During this epoch, for the most part, men and women did
not enjoy rights as individuals but as participants in corporations and institutions. People received their identity
as members of guilds, religious orders, noble families,
universities, or as serfs working on a particular estate.
Each group had its separate judicial system. Clerics were
tried in Church courts and manorial courts decided cases
involving serfs.

However, in theory, the concept of human rights
based on natural law was accepted by most theologians
in the Middle Ages. The idea that all men are equal in
the eyes of God (if nowhere else) was put forward by
almost all medieval philosophers. Perhaps the greatest
theologian of this period, St. Thomas Aquinas (1225-
1274), believed that men had the right to disobey man-
made legislation which violated the "eternal principles
of law." The Church even upheld the right to murder a
tyrannical monarch if he grossly violated the rights of
his subjects. Thus, many theologians upheld the right
of a religious fanatic who murdered King Henry IV of
France in 1610 when he fell out of favor with the Catholic Church.

**Medieval England.** Great Britain is the European
country from which our modern concept of human
rights is largely derived. The Anglo-Saxons who settled in
Britain, more than any other branch of the Germanic
peoples, kept alive the sense of personal rights and liberties which the Roman historian Tacitus described as
characteristic of the early Germans. During the Middle
Ages, alongside of and within the militaristic framework
of feudalism, the English people maintained at least some
of the fundamentals of self-government. The National
Assembly—composed of the leading dignataries of the

realm, both clerical and lay—the "Moot of the Wise men" or *Witanagemot* at one time had the outer markings at least of the later parliament.

One of the great landmarks in the protection of the individual from arbitrary government was the Magna Charta which a group of English nobles forced King John to sign in 1215. This document *(see Reading No. 6)* set forth the fundamental principle that neither king nor baronage but the law of the land should be supreme in the realm. This concept laid the groundwork for the great advances in human rights which were to come in England in the following centuries. To some degree all classes shared in the benefits of Magna Charta. The Church, the towns, the merchant class, and the serfs were all provided with certain guarantees. Of particular importance were the provisions which protected due process of law and freedom from arbitrary action by the crown. Later British monaarchs were required to take an oath to uphold the Magna Charta.

Over the centuries English monarchs were also obliged to take account of the growing power of Parliament. The precise development of Parliament is obscured by the shifting meaning of the terms used in contemporary records. But by the thirteenth century, it emerged as a national institution. A further important development occurred when the Parliament of 1295 summoned two knights of the shire to represent the minor gentry and two burgesses from every borough to represent the rising business class. By 1340, these elements met separately to form the House of Commons which gradually over the centuries has come to represent a greater and greater portion of the common people of the country. The fourteenth century also saw the establishment of the principle that new taxes required Parliament's approval. By 1414, the Commons took the important step of drawing up petitions in the exact terms in which they wished to have them granted. That is, they outlined in a "bill" of Parliament the "act" which the king should make law by giving his signature.

**England Under the Tudors**. After fifteenth century England had been ravaged by the War of the Roses, the Tudor dynasty, beginning with Henry VII in 1485, re-established royal authority. Henry forced the barons to accept the authority of the royal Star Chamber Court and imposed forced loans on them. But despite the renewed power of the monarchy under Henry VII and his son, Henry VIII, the pattern of English history never wholly lost its unique design, that of ordered liberty under the reign of law. Though Henry VIII was tempted to assert personal rule without regard to the traditional forms of the constitution, he ultimately found it more to his advantage to rule through existing institutions. Despite the murder of an estimated 72,000 people, Parliament survived the reign of Henry VIII. Under Elizabeth I, England enjoyed great prosperity which helped to insure her popularity. During this period England made important contributions to Western civilization. Elizabeth and her advisers built up an efficient central administration which left little for the Legislature to do. But the Queen's Ministers were careful not to flaunt their authority in disregard of Parliament.

**The Struggle Against the Stuarts**. After the death of Queen Elizabeth in 1603, James I ascended the throne and reigned from 1603 to 1625, thus beginning the ill-fated Stuart dynasty. James' son, Charles I, who reigned from 1625 to 1649, attempted to govern, raise money, and secure uniformity in religion in disregard of the rights of Parliament and many of the traditional limitations on the power of the crown. These actions initiated a complex religious and political struggle that lasted nearly a century. It was marked by episodes of civil war, military dictatorship, religious persecution, judicial murder, and the violent deposition of two kings. In this process the English decided what their vital rights were. A particular discovery was that political or constitutional rights were interdependent with personal and civil rights, neither being able to survive without the other. In previous periods, Englishmen's rights had been left vague and ambiguous, the crown being generally trusted not to abuse its powers. A large reservoir of government authority was thought necessary for the common good. But when the Stuarts began to stretch those powers, their definition became a burning question. For instance, the Magna Charta clause on "scutages and aids" *(see Reading No. 6)* was interpreted to mean no taxation save by vote of Parliament. But the king was also recognized to have other lawful means of raising money. One of them was "ship-money," an arbitrary exaction on seacoast towns for aid in naval emergencies. Charles I, claiming (with considerable reason) that he needed money to increase the navy, extended the levy to the inland counties as well and collected it in time of peace. The law was unclear whether this violated the Magna Charta or not.

Similar controversies arose in regard to criminal justice when the Stuarts tried to punish their opponents. Magna Charta's clause on "judgement by one's peers" was interpreted to guarantee trial by jury. Furthermore, it had become customary to hold criminal trials under so-called common law, which gave the accused important protections, including prohibition of self-incrimination, and of torture. But there was also a long-recognized criminal jurisdiction over certain offenses by the King's Council (known as the "Court of Star Chamber"), which respected none of the common law rules. For over a century, Star Chamber had been extremely important in maintaining public order. A further important right under common law was the Writ of Habeas Corpus, commanding that anyone holding someone in confinement must give an adequate reason for doing so to the royal courts. This was originally devised to prevent imprisonment without trial in the local jurisdictions of powerful noblemen. But it had uncertain application to royal jails, and to hold a prisoner simply "by special order of the King's council" had been considered in some instances as perfectly legal. A further vital issue was the nature of the judiciary itself.

In strict theory, the judges were only the king's personal servants, dismissable at his pleasure, although ordinarily they were highly independent, and held office for life. But under the Stuarts, judges whose decisions displeased the king might be dismissed summarily, which made nonsense of any idea of rights under law.

Moreover, in this long controversy, it was often unclear which was the side of right and law. Often the Stuart's enemies seemed to aspire to be worse tyrants than they (especially in regard to religious persecution), and it was rather the royal cause that stood for freedom and justice. Many persons were also led to support the dynasty simply out of the instinctual medieval fear of insubordination. Given the nature of man, how far could one relax the power and majesty of constitutional authority without inviting the dissolution of society, without which all questions of rights were meaningless? Most experience had shown that rebellion against the established order of things committed more wrong than it remedied. After the dismal dictatorship of Oliver Cromwell (1599-1658), most Englishmen were convinced of this more than ever. Under Charles II (1630-1685), probably a majority of Englishmen subscribed to the doctrine of the "divine right of kings," that is, that their authority came directly from God, and in no way from human action, and that to resist a lawful king, even if he were a tyrant, was a deadly sin.

**The Glorious Revolution.**   An important stage in resolving the conflict, and one of the most significant events in the history of human rights, was the deposition of King James II in November, 1688. By various blunders and excesses James had managed to unite against him nearly everyone in England, including the adherents of divine-right theory, and for once the whole country was able to work together. Quckly a new Parliament chose as his successors William and Mary (his daughter and her husband, ruling jointly). They had no title save through vote of Parliament, thus establishing the principle that the

crown was subordinate to the nation. The new regime
soon enacted important restrictions on the royal power
and fundamental guarantees of the political and personal
rights of individuals. The new order was very successful.
It secured the obedience of the country without recourse
to force and 1688 turned out to be England's last revolution. It also enjoyed economic prosperity and military
victory and, by 1715, England was recognized as a leading
world power.

The new regime was concerned to establish its own
legitimacy. Here it found useful the recently published
views of the philosopher John Locke (1632-1704). *(See
Reading No. 7.)* Locke took basically a utilitarian view of
society, omitting any idea of its divine or suprarational
origin. He theorized that society had been founded by
unattached individuals in a "state of nature," in order to
protect their interests, of which the chief were life,
liberty, and property. They, therefore, had contracted
among themselves to obey a government, to which each
resigned his rights of self-protection. But the government
was itself under a contract, being created only to look
after the interest of the members. If it did not perform
this obligation, it no longer had a right to obedience, and
its subjects were free to choose another. It is unthinkable
that they could have made an agreement to allow their
ruler to do them unlimited harm, without any power of
redress. Locke then proceeded to argue that revolution, if
carried out responsibly, was not as dangerous as commonly supposed.

The novelty of Locke lay not in basing government on
a contract between ruler and ruled, (which was implicit
in Magna Charta), but in providing for its termination
in the event of nonperformance, that is to say, the right of
revolution. His views were taken as virtually the official
explanation of the Glorious Revolution. As Parliament
decreed within weeks of James's ouster, King James,
"having broken the original contract between king and
people," had "abdicated." The throne, therefore, was

vacant, and it was legal to elect William and Mary. Parliament was careful to insist that the king, and not the revolutionaries, was the one who had broken the law. The Lockean view of revolution was widely accepted in the eighteenth century and used to justify both the American and French Revolutions.

In the next few years the revolutionary regime passed much new legislation to prevent the Stuart abuses from recurring. (Some were already in force; *e.g.*, Star Chamber had been abolished in 1641, the Habeas Corpus Act had been passed in 1679.) This new legislation concerned a miscellany of constituional definitions, personal rights, legal reforms, and religious measures. This is to be seen in the Bill of Rights (1689). *(See Reading No. 8, which sums up Jame's worst misdeeds.)* This wide range reflects the hard-won experience that there could be no free government save in a society of free individuals, and vice versa, which is the central principle of modern democracy.

The first step was to subordinate the crown to Parliament. The king could not maintain an army, raise money, or dispense from the laws without its consent, nor was he allowed to interfere wiith the operations of Parliament. In the sphere of individual rights, all criminal justice was put under the limitations of common law, including trial by jury, Habeas Corpus, and the prohibition of arbitrary imprisonment or excessive bail. Treason, an accusation that had been greatly abused, was made far more difficult to prove (1696). Judges were given life tenure (1701).

In 1695 there was added a new right found indispensable to political and religions liberty—freedom of the press. This had been advocated eloquently in the 1640s by the eminent John Milton (1608-1674), in his *Aeropagitica. (See Reading No. 9.)* In the general confusion of that time, the governmental power of censorship had virtually ceased, allowing the publication of an enormous variety of opinions, especially in religion. Many of the Puritan clergy, still thinking on essentially medieval lines of authority and conformity, asked for the restoration of censorship of the press. Milton retored that it ill be-seemed people who had lately been passionately denouncing the Stuarts' censorship to seek to impose one of their own. Furthermore, and more important, the right freely to seek the truth was absolutely fundamental to Christianity and human dignity, and it was totally mistaken to try to define it by law. In fact, from the 1640s forward it was difficult for any English government to censor the press, and in 1695 the last "Licensing Act" was simply allowed to expire.

**Religious Freedom.** A great landmark in the realization of human rights in the spiritual realm was the Toleration Act of 1689. Its scope was limited; it only gave freedom of worship to certain of the dissenting Protestants, and otherwise left all non-Anglicans as second-class citizens, excluded from all public employment and subject to other disabilities. But its effect was broader than its terms, for in fact the crown soon ceased all attempts at religious persecution. Essentially, government had become more self-confident, feeling less need for the support of a monopolistic state church, and finding that attempting to enforce religious uniformity was a source of weakness rather than strength. In toleration England was following a general trend, having been anticipated by the Dutch and by its own North American colonies.

These points had been made clear years before by perhaps the best known advocate of religious toleration, Roger Williams (1603-1683). Williams had been expelled for religious dissent from Massachusetts by the Puritan clergy, after which he founded the colony of Rhode Island in 1636. This was probably the first place in the world where complete religious freedom was the law of the land. While in England to obtain a charter for Rhode Island, Williams wrote *The Bloody Tenent of Persecution* (1644). *(See Reading No. 10.)* It was directed at the Massachusetts clergy as much as at the English. His first point was that to compel consciences by law was totally contrary to the spirit of the Gospel, and would only succeed in producing liars and hypocrites. But he went on to recognize that the task of civil government was outside the scope of religion and that even infidel and heathen regimes were as truly governments as Christian ones. It was necessary not only to liberate conscience from government, but also to free government from the need to take sides in questions of religion, so that it could treat all its citizens fairly. In this recognition of the need to separate public affairs from religion, Williams was prophetic of one of the key points of the Enlightenment.

Religious toleration had great symbolic importance. In the seventeenth century nearly everyone took religion very seriously and sincerely believed that his own church was the only true one. To allow "false" religions to function, if one had the capability to suppress them, seemed disloyal to one's own faith. Therefore, toleration meant a real sacrifice of deep convictions, a recognition of the rights owed to the consciences of other people, simply because they were human beings. The fact that government now guaranteed the rights of the indivudal in something as fundamental and cherished as religion and declared that here was an area of human dignity in which no outside authority had any jurisdiction whatever, was a powerful precedent for similar treatment in other respects.

# 4

# THE AMERICAN AND FRENCH REVOLUTIONS

**The Enlightenment**. In the history of Western civilization, there have been sporadic oscillations between periods when men's minds were influenced by reason, and other epochs when romanticism and irrationality pervaded the intellectual landscape. The eighteenth century, often referred to as the "Age of Enlightenment," ranks with the Renaissance as an example of an era when the spirit of free inquiry played a substantial if precarious role in human affairs.

At the core of the Enlightenment was a belief in the perfectability and decency of mankind. Eighteenth-century *"philosophes"* rejected the idea of original sin. The Christian dogma of the essential depravity of fallen humanity because of original sin was the basis of ecclesiastical authority. But the enlightened thinkers took a much more optimistic view of man's fundamental nature and inclinations. They were forced to admit that the world was full of evil and corruption but they denied that this was the inevitable outgrowth of humanity's basic depravity. Jean Jacques Rousseau (1712-1778), in his *Social Contract,* argued that if there was much evil in the world it could not be blamed on man's natural inclinations but on social injustice and inequality which drove man to commit every conceivable depraved act.

The men of the Enlightenment came predominantly from the middle class or petty nobility and as such favored reforms in society which would limit the excessive privileges of the aristocracy. Francois Marie Voltaire (1694-1778) argued persuasively for freedom of person, the press, and religious thought. He also favored the abolition of serfdom and the reform of criminal law. But like most of the *philosophes,* Voltaire stopped short of advocating a democratic republic. Many intellectuals of this period favored an enlightened despotism which would be a monarchy where the ruler took account of the interests of all his subjects. It was believed that such an enlightened despotism was the proper way to govern, taking into account the nature of man and the origin of society.

The impetus for the Enlightenment came from the scientific discoveries of the seventeenth century. Newtonian physics was based on a system of natural physical laws for the entire universe. For the *philosophes,* a logical outgrowth of Newtonian natural law was the concept of natural rights which were the common heritage of all mankind. The *philosophes* did not originate this theory of the inalienable rights of man but they made it their fundamental ethical and social gospel and introduced it into practical politics which had a profound effect on the eigtheenth-century revolutions.

In the area of religion the *philosophes* attacked all dogmas which they considered obscure, incomprehensible, and absurd. The enlightened thinkers criticized the Church as priestcraft and as an impediment to intellectual progress. Although their religious beliefs differed considerably, the *philosophes* generally favored a form of natural religion based on the common ideas of morality which they believed were engraved on the hearts of all men. They believed that stripped of their supernatural and mysterious envelope, all the major religions of the world were a reflection of this universal natural religion which had as its core the worship of God and a common sense moral code. One of their chief criticisms of Christianity was that by inspiring fear of an invisible tyrant it had made men slavish and cowardly toward kings and incapable of managing their own affairs.

**The Eighteenth-Century Revolutions.** Many of the ideas of the Enlightenment were put into practice in the wave of revolutionary agitation which swept Western civilization in the late eighteenth century. Although this revolutionary impulse took a different form in each country, there were certain common features. In general, eighteenth-century revolutions signified a reaction against aristocratic privilege. Most commoners, particularly the rising middle classes, were no longer content to submit to kings and pretentious nobles. On a political level, the eighteenth-century revolutions opposed the exercise of public power by a closed system which did not receive its power from the people. One of the chief aims of the revolutionaries was the establishment of governmental bodies which would be popularly elected and serve the interests of a wider cross section of the nation. Many nations were affected by the impetus toward revolution in the late eighteenth century including Belgium, Italy, Germany, and several countries in Latin America. The two most important manifestations of the eighteenth-century revolutions were in America and France.

**The American Revolution.** The first major upheaval of the late eighteenth century was the American Revolution. It has been argued that no genuine revolution took place in America since all that happened was a conservative defense of established rights against British encroachment. But along with the movements for independence, the Americans implemented many revolutionary reforms which are noticeable in the numerous statues and declarations issued by Virginia *(see Reading No. 11)* and other colonies. Such concepts as the rights of man, the social contract, popular sovereignty, written constitutions, religious freedom, separation of powers, and freedom of thought and speech were transported by the American Revolution from the realm of speculation into concrete action. The basic documents of the American Revolution clearly reflect the ideas on human rights which had been developed in British constitutional history and the Enlightenment.

**The Declaration of Independence.** The American Revolution began as a dispute between Britain and her North American colonies over Parliament's right to levy taxes to pay for Imperial defense. Very soon, however, radicals in the colonies began to agitate against numerous other British injustices and in favor of greater freedom for the colonies. In January 1776 Thomas Paine (1737-1809), a recent arrival from Great Britain, wrote *Common Sense* as a means of persuading the colonists that the solution to their problems was independence from Britain. Paine, an avowed republican, had no hesitation in attacking the concept of monarchy and the person of George III.

Somewhat later, on July 4, 1776, the American Congress voted to approve the Declaration of Independence. *(See Reading No. 12.)* The principal author of this document, Thomas Jefferson (1743-1826), was greatly influenced by the political thought of John Locke who had held that when a monarch did not uphold the "natural rights" of his subjects, the people had the right to depose him. The Declaration accused George III of violating the basic rights which the American colonists believed they enjoyed as British subjects. But most significant of all was the fact that the American Declaration broadened these concepts from being the prescription rights of Englishmen into human rights of universal application.

**The Constitution of the United States.** The most important idea to emerge from the American Revolution was the concept of the people as the constituent power. The Constitution of 1789, which inaugurated the new government, was drafted by a constitutional convention which in theory embodied the sovereignty of the people. The convention was chosen for a specific purpose, not to govern but to set up the institutions of a new government. When its work was complete, the convention disbanded and the Constitution had to be ratified by the sovereign people.

Under the rule of the Constitution, all government was limited government. Bounds were set by the Constitution which could not be transgressed by any public authority. Two levels of law were recognized under the system. There was a higher law, *i.e.,* the Constitution itself, that could only be amended or changed by the people through constitutional conventions or similar bodies. There was also statutory law which could be made or unmade within the proscribed limits by legislators who were delegated this power by the Constitution.

The Constitution of 1787 contains guarantees of some basic human rights. It specifically protests the writ of Habeas Corpus from suspension except in very limited situations. Also protected are freedom to debate in Congress and freedom of movement. Bills of attainder are specifically prohibited by the Constitution. However, despite these protections, many people in the new country felt a need for further human rights guarantees. Thus in 1791, a Bill of Rights *(see Reading No. 13)* was added to the Constitution; it incorporated most of the traditional "rights of Englishmen" and established some limits to Congressional legislation.

**The French Revolution**. The human rights concepts of the Enlightenment and the example of the American Revolution had a profound influence on the men who made the French Revolution. Many of the reforms advocated by the philosophers were implemented in France during the period after 1789. The codification of the law which was advocated by Voltaire was eventually completed by Napoleon (1769-1821). Other basic reforms of the revolutionary era were the secularization of the state and the extension of civil rights to non-Catholics. The elimination of torture from judicial proceedings marked a major triumph of the Enlightenment spirit. The French Revolution also saw the inauguration of a campaign for the abolition of both slavery and the slave trade which was not completed however until 1848.

From the American Revolution, the French borrowed the idea of the people as a constituent power. The French Constituent Assembly was copied after the federal and state conventions in the United States. In this process the people dissolve the present governmental structures and in theory revert to a "state of nature." Then they create a new governmental structure with new offices and authorities and endowed them with written grants of power. This was in a judicial sense the very essence of revolution, the practical acting out of the social contract and the assertion of the sovereignty of the people. Moreover, it represented the practical application of the concept of natural law.

**The Declaration of the Rights of Man and the Citizen.**  On August 27, 1789, the French Constituent Assembly passed the Declaration of the Rights of Man and the Citizen. *(See Reading No. 1.)* This declaration contains most of the reform program demanded by Enlightenment thinkers in the eighteenth century. Of the *philosophes,* the one whose influence is most notable is Rousseau. Article VI of the document stated his famous formula: "Law is the expression of the general will." The declaration recognizes that the rights of man were the heritage of humanity before any society or State had come into being. According to Article II, the conservation of man's natural rights is the aim of any political association. Article I declared that "Men are born and remain free and equal in their rights." These rights are defined as liberty, property, personal safety, and the right to resist oppression. The declaration also recognized equality before the law, repudiation of all hereditary privilege, national sovereignty, accountability of public officials, freedom of speech and press, and the separation of government powers. Conspicuously absent was a provision for civil equality for non-Catholics. This important omission was necessitated by tactical considerations because the revolutionary leaders still needed the support of certain clerical elements.

**Edmund Burke.**  The Revolution in France was not without its critics. Chief among these was Edmund Burke (1729-1797), a member of the British Parliament, who in 1790 published his *Reflections on the Revolution in France. (See Reading No. 14.)* Burke took issue with what he called the "school of the rights of men." As a devout Christian, he upheld the concept of natural law derived from the will of God. But Bruke believed that while man had certain rights in the original "state of nature," these had no practical bearing on the condition of men in existing society. Man's natural rights do not apply to citizens living under legitimate constitutional government. In any actual society, man's rights derive from his relation to other men. Thus, a person's station in life (noble or commoner), his wealth (rich or poor), his education (learned or illiterate), determine his rights as well as his obligations. Burke's volume created a great sensation in the England of his day. It triggered a great public debate in which numerous books and pamphlets were written both to support and attack his point of view.

**Thomas Paine and "The Rights of Man".** Burke's most famous adversary was Thomas Paine. In 1791 Paine wrote *The Rights of Man,* Part I *(see Reading No. 15)* which was meant as a reply to Burke. Paine argued that man's natural rights do affect his status. In society natural rights are translated into and are the basis for civil rights which are the due of every individual. Paine supported the idea of social compact since he believed that the only legitimate government was one where individuals come together "each in his own personal and right" to form a new government. All power in society flows from the consent of the governed who have the right to replace a corrupt or inefficient ruler. Paine's *Rights of Man* was regarded as a basic text by the radical forces in England.

**Declaration of the Rights of Man of 1793.** Another rallying point of the left was the French Constitution of 1793 and a revised Declaration of the Rights of Man, which served as its preamble. This new constitution was written when the French Revolution entered a more radical stage. After the monarchy was overthrown, France found herself at war with much of Europe. A republic was established in September 1792. The 1793 constitution provided for a democratic system in which all male citizens could vote. The Declaration of Rights which served as a preamble to the constitution went beyond the 1789 document. It stated that "the aim of society is happiness for all." It provided for the right of the people to work, public assistance, and mass education. It recognized not only the right to resist oppression but also the right to rise in insurrection. While the Declaration of Rights of 1789 became the basis of the human rights program of the middle class, it is not hard to understand why the Declaration of 1793 became a symbol of the human rights aspirations of the less privileged order.

**Napoleon.** The French Revolution went through a number of stages until General Napoleon Bonaparte proclaimed the French Empire in 1804 with himself as monarch. Napoleon ruled in the name of the revolution and attempted to consolidate many of its gains. Though he rejected the democratic principles of 1793, he retained many of the original gains of 1789. The Napoleonic Code of 1804 supported the liberty of conscience and employment, provided for the abolition of feudalism, and retained the property rights and rights of citizenship bequeathed by the revolutionairies of 1789. The Napoleonic Wars spread many of the ideas of the French Revolution throughout Europe. The French propagated such concepts as equality before the law, civil marriage, secular education, abolition of feudalism, and abolition of aristocratic privilege. Even after Napoleon was defeated, the Old Regime could not be easily reestablished in Europe.

**The Congress of Vienna.** In 1814, members of the victorious coalition which had defeated Napoleon met in Vienna to decide the fate of Europe. Despite their opposition to the principles of the Revolutionary Era, the delegates to the Vienna Congress laid down a great variety of provisions on human rights. In the united state formed by Belgium and Holland, religious liberty was guaranteeed by the Great Powers. In the new Confederation of German States, religious liberty and civil rights for the Jews were provided for in the Federal Constitution. The rights of the Polish minority in Prussia, Austria, and Russia were also guaranteed by the Congress. But the most important human rights topic discussed at the Vienna Congress was slavery which remained one of the great blots on Western civilization.

# 5

# THE FIGHT AGAINST SLAVERY

**The Slave Trade.** The slave trade began on a large scale in the sixteenth century when the colonization of the New World created a vast market for African blacks who could work long hours in the hot sun. Slaves were transported from Africa to the Spanish, Portugese, and English colonies in the West Indies and South America. The inhumanity of the slave trade was staggering. Human beings were reduced to cargo. The mortality rate was high from disease, maltreatment, and suicide. *(See Reading No. 16.)*

Slave ships from England, Spain, Portugal, and occasionally Denmark, France, and the Netherlands sailed the East Coast of Africa buying their victims from African middlemen with cloth, iron, gunpowder, weapons, and other Western goods that were relatively cheap in Europe. Those captives who survived the subsequent Middle Passage across the ocean were sold and new cargo from the Americas was transported back. This provided profit on all parts of the journey.

The tremendous slave trade was fed by early attitudes toward slaves. It was considered cheaper to work them very hard and replace them every few years than to care well for them. This plus the ever-widening circle of settled land in the colonies created a voracious appetite for slaves. It has been estimated that at least 421,400 slaves were imported in the sixteenth century, 1,341,100 in the seventeenth century, and over 6,000,000 in the eighteenth. Despite the treaties prohibiting the slave trade, it is believed that nearly two million slaves were brought into the New World between 1810 and 1870.

**Slavery in Latin America.** When the Spanish and Portugese came to the New World, they found most of the territory inhabited by various Indian tribes who were cruelly decimated by the conquistadors and ravaged by the white man's diseases. It proved necessary to import

blacks to work on the plantations and in the mines.
Fortunately, in Latin America there were certain institutions which allowed the black slaves some limited rights.
The Catholic Church mandated that slaves could not work
on Sundays and religious holidays. Slaves were sometimes
allowed to buy their freedom. In Brazil, there was a system of *negros de ganho* who enjoyed semi-independence.
These artisans worked in various trades for wages, part
of which they were obliged to give to their owners and
a portion of which they could keep for themselves. But
the vast majority of African blacks lived under the most
brutal conditions and their mortality rate was high.

**Abolition of Slavery in England.** In eighteenth-
century England, there was considerable agitation against
slavery and all its brutality. In particular, there was opposition to the importation of slaves into the British Isles.
The issue at dispute was whether blacks resident in the
country were entitled to the protection of English law
which prohibited slavery. This question was put to the
test by the noted abolitionist Granville Sharp (1735-
1813) in a case involving a West Indian slave, Jonathan
Strong, brought to England by his master, David Lisle.
Strong was beaten and abandoned by Lisle but upon finding the slave again two years later, he reenslaved him and
sold him to another West Indian planter. While awaiting
transport back to the Indies, Strong was put in an English
jail without warrant or charge. Sharp secured the black
man's legal freedom since he had committed no jailable
offense under English law. Sharp successfully argued
that the human rights protected under English law were
applicable to all humans in England.

Sharp's legal battles in similar cases culminated in 1772
with the Somerset decision, which was popularly interpreted to mean "free soil, free men." Somerset, another
West Indian slave, had tried to escape while in England
but was unsuccessful. Before he could be shipped out of
England, Sharp served a writ of Habeas Corpus on the
captain of the ship and the matter went to court. It was

finally ruled that since a slave was not a thing, but a human being, he was protected by all the rights of all the subjects of the same king. Although this effectively ended slavery within England, it did not affect the status of slaves in the British colonies or the traffic in human flesh.

**Abolition of the Slave Trade**. After the abolition of slavery in England, the focus of the abolitionist movement was turned to the slave trade. The inhumanity of the slave trade was amply demonstrated by the case of the *Zong* (1781). Her inept captain, suffering heavy losses in crew and cargo, jettisoned 135 unprofitable slaves overboard. The resulting legal controversy ranged not over the murder of 135 human beings, but over the insurance liability and whether this had been a proper action by the captain for the safety of the ship, or a ploy to collect the insurance money. In its decision, the court ruled that the question was not whether the cargo was human or not, but whether the captain had the right to jettison the cargo. Further appeals could deal only with this point.

After the *Zong* decision, various groups were formed in order to agitate against the slave trade. Many abolitionists believed that if they eliminated the slave trade, most of the abuses of slavery would be curtailed. Without a continuous source of slaves, owners would be forced to care well for the ones already in their possession. It was also felt that the possibility of success was greater for a more limited action than for total aboliton.

The fight for abolition was led by William Wilberforce (1759–1833) and his supporters. Many of these abolitionists were practicing politicans with some power and prestige to support their efforts. But despite the efforts of Thomas Clarkson (1760–1846), Charles James Fox (1749–1806), and William Pitt the Younger (1759–1806) there was much opposition to the abolition of the slave trade. Pitt, Prime Minister, 1783–1801 and 1804–1806, was restricted by his position, although his support and friendship with Wilberforce were well known.

A central focus of the antislavery campaign of this period was the assertion that blacks were human and could not be treated as property or cargo. The famous medallion struck by Josiah Wedgewood (1730-1795) in 1786 depicted a suppliant Negro slave and bore the inscription "AM I NOT A MAN AND A BROTHER?" Those who supported the slave trade spread false stories about its economic necessity to the country. During a lengthy investigation of the slave trade by the Privy Council, many witnesses perjured themselves by giving false testimony of the benevolent treatment of blacks on slave ships and on West Indian plantations. But slowly, because of the antislavery agitation and because of the decline of the West Indies as a source of colonial wealth for Great Britain, the movement for abolition of the slave trade gained momentum.

Finally, on March 25, 1807, it became illegal for British subjects to engage in the slave trade. The United States followed suit in 1808. However, this gesture made during the Napoleonic Wars was meaningless without the agreement of other maritime powers. A significant step was taken at the Congress of Vienna on February 8, 1815, when an agreement was produced which condemned the slave trade. But it took several more years before the Spanish and Portugese would sign treaties abolishing the commerce in human flesh.

**Abolition of Slavery in the West Indies.** The next obvious step for the abolitionist movement was the end of slavery in the West Indies. Because of economic considerations this did not prove to be an easy task. The slave owners insisted that they must be reimbursed for the loss of their slaves. Eventually, at a cost to the British taxpayer of 20 million pounds, a bill was passed which provided for the gradual emancipation of slaves in the West Indies. The final proposal introduced by Lord Granville (1759-1834) in 1833 and passed by Parliament called for the long-term apprenticeship for the freed slaves. Since most slaves in the West Indies performed only field labor, this meant that a slave would have to spend many more years learning the menial task he had already been doing for a lifetime. This system quickly broke down since once they had tasted freedom the West Indian blacks would no longer accept *de facto* slavery.

**Slavery in Early America.** Slaves were introduced in the English colonies in 1642. There were a few black slaves in early New England where their treatment on the whole tended to be relatively humane. In Massachusetts, for example, laws regarding slavery were based on Mosaic law. As in the Old Testament, these laws recognized the slave as a human being first, as property secondly. They regarded slavery as a personal misfortune, not as evidence of inherent inferiority, and in no way interfered with the possibility of being one of God's elect. Since these laws recognized the humanity of a slave, certain rights were allowed. The slave could own property, be a witness against white men, be tried by juries, and sue in regular courts. This last provision enabled slaves to sue for their freedom if there was doubt about the validity of the master's title. The key to this religious philosophy was the *Bible*, which all religious men should know, including slaves. Some education was provided to enable the slave to study the *Bible* and become a full religious member of the community.

In the early South, slavery was not an all-important factor in the economy. Many early Revolutionary War leaders such as Washington and Jefferson favored some form of gradual emancipation. There was little opposition in the South to the Constitutional provision that the importation of slaves would end in twenty years. However, with the invention of the cotton gin in 1793 and its gradual widespread use, slavery became much more lucrative and the South tended to more rigidly defend its "peculiar institution."

**The Abolitionist Movement in the United States.** As slavery became more entrenched in the South, the abolitionist movement grew in the North. The abolition movement was, in many cases, tied in with a general religious revival and reform movement that was sweeping America in the first half of the nineteenth century. Many of the most noted abolitionists started their fight for equal rights in the women's rights movement along with concern for universal education and utopian communities. This was an era of social experimentation and reexamination of the rights and relationships of man, his God, and country.

To many, the symbol of the new wave of determined abolitionists was William Lloyd Garrison (1805-1879) and his followers Wendell Phillips (1811-1884) and John Rankin (1795-1886). *(See Reading No. 17).* Garrison's philosophy was amply stated in the weekly newspaper, the LIBERATOR, which he founded in 1831. Although not the largest of the antislavery publications, it appeared to be the most influential and drew the most wrath from Southerners.

The growing antislavery press terrified the South. They feared that with any encouragement at all there would be mass slave insurrections. The South instituted militant efforts, including legislation and mob action, to censor severely all written materials coming from the North. Southern politicians were also successful in obtaining a House of Representatives gag rule on the question of slavery petitions (1840).

The increased Northern efforts to aid fugitive slaves and agitation for the end of slavery drew reaction in the South. Fearful of the growing number of freed slaves within their borders and spreading knowledge of outside efforts to aid fugitives, Southerners placed additional limitations on blacks. Manumission was forbidden in some states, freed slaves were forbidden residence in others, and professional fugitive hunters became common. Radicals encouraged the kidnapping of abolitionists by placing a price on their heads.

These actions by Southerners were perceived by Northerners as limiting the rights secured by all under the

Consitution and forced many neutral observers into
the fight on the side of the abolitionists. Most notable
of these was John Quincy Adams (1767-1848), former
President of the United States, later a member of the
House of Representatives. Adams may have been neutral
about the slavery question but he was enraged by the
Southern atacks on Northern rights and fought the gag
rule in Congress.

Southerners, in turn, perceived Northern action as an
attack on their way of life and their property rights in
slaves guaranteed by the same Constitution. Thus the
fight over slavery became a sectional dispute and a fight
over the preservation of the Union and not of the preservation of black people. Indeed, there were large segments
of the abolitionist movement which felt strongly that
slavery was morally wrong yet did not consider the black
person to be the equal of the white. The fight was to
end slavery but not to necessarily make the freed slave a
citizen. The removal of black people from the United
States after the termination of slavery was seriously proposed by many abolitionists. It was felt that blacks were
of such a level of civilization and natural tendency as to
make living in the same land with whites impossible.
Despite the proliferation of vocal former slaves, blacks
were never asked what they hoped for after slavery.

**Black Abolitionists.** In the United States as in
England, blacks played a key role in the abolitionist
movement. Their courage was incredible. Freedom in no
way secured for them equal rights with the white man.
Despite differing views on slavery, the North and the
South had basically the same attitude toward the Negro
as an individual. Prejudice prevented even skilled blacks
from obtaining decent, if any, employment. Many freed
men were untrained, ill, poorly educated, and far from
friends and family. Yet, despite status not much above
that of a slave, they wrote, lectured, lobbied, and fought
for abolition. Many illiterate and poverty-stricken freed-
men skimped on food and other essentials to buy relatives
out of slavery.

Paul Cuffe( ? - 1817), born free, was a successful seaman, merchant, and Quaker. He pioneered colonization efforts in Sierra Leone. This widely considered solution to the emancipation "problem" was seldom supported with such practical efforts. Cuffe paid the expenses for thirty-eight settlers and gave continued support to the concept.

One of the most remarkable black fighters was Harriet Tubman (1821-1913), an illiterate fugitive slave. She personally executed forays into the Deep South to lead slaves through the Underground Railroad to free states and Canada. She financed much of this effort herself by working as a cook. During the Civil War she worked as a nurse and spy behind Confederate lines. After emancipation, she continued to fight for the basic rights of her people, especially for education and homes for the elderly.

Most of the black abolitionists are known through their narratives of captivity. This genre was an important intellectual weapon as well as a dramatic and horrifying chronicle. Such tales were highly popular and were sold at antislavery meetings, sometimes by the authors themselves. They were often tied in with lectures by the authors and the proceeds were used to buy freedom for families of the authors or to finance antislavery organizations' efforts.

Among the most famous and extensive of these narratives were those written by Frederick Douglass (1817?-1895). *(See Reading No. 18.)* Douglass fought his way from slavery to the position of a respected United States diplomat. He lectured widely and published the antislavery weekly "North Star." During the Civil War he helped organize two black regiments.

William Wells Brown (1816-1864) became America's first black novelist (1853) and playwright (1858) but was born a slave. After his own escape he worked on a Great Lakes steamer and aided many other fleeing slaves. He travelled and lectured widely in Europe against slavery. European friends raised money to ransom him so he could return to America a free man. Despite his Doctor of Divinity Degree from Heidelberg, W.C. Pennington as a fugitive slave could not safely return home. British abolitionists investigated the possibility of legal immunity if he returned to American after swearing allegiance to the British crown. But without the assurance of British protection if he was seized, they decided instead to raise the money to buy his freedom. As with other black abolitionists, his works were published in England. Henry Highland Garnet escaped from slavery with his family in 1824 and managed to get an excellent education at Oneida Institute and became pastor of a Troy, New York, Presbyterian Church. He, too, made the grand tour of Europe to preach against slavery. In this country his remarks addressed to slaves called for revolt.

**Civil War and Reconstruction**. In the United States, the issue of slavery was decided by the Civil War. During that conflict President Lincoln issued the Emancipation Proclamation. It declared that slaves in any state in rebellion against the Union were to be free. The Proclamation did not free any slaves in the slave states that remained part of the Union. Most slaves were not freed until the Union victory in 1865. After the war, three Amendments were added to the Constitution *(See Reading No. 19)* which eventually banned slavery in fact as well as in law.

Freedom is an elusive word and the freedom granted by the Thirteenth Amendment was particularly elusive. It removed actual ownership of blacks but did absolutely nothing else to secure for them basic civil and political rights. Even free blacks had always been subject to legal restrictions as to where they could move freely, live, be employed, eat, sleep, and pray. The newly freed slaves were immediately subject to all these restrictions on their personal liberty. The freeing of slaves without any additional provision had the effect of totally abandoning them rather than freeing them. Most were illiterate, with no occupational training, living in a war-ravaged land. Burned farms and business could not provide employement even for trained freemen. This left the turned-out slave with no home or food, the most necessary of all human needs. This also left him a stranger in a strange land for although he may have now been considered a person, he was a legal nonentity, with the status of a foreigner, but without the government of a homeland to protect his rights. Although this was theoretically corrected by passage of the Fourteenth Amendment in 1868, which made the former slave a citizen, in reality little was changed. Even with the right to vote, the black was still subject to segretationist laws. This legislation denied his equality as a human being in every way. Basic sustenance items such as housing, the right to eat in public, were denied or offered in altered form. Public access and freedom to congregate, day or night, was denied. Legal sanctions for real or imagined offenses were much harsher than for whites. Even the right to die was legislated. Blacks could not be admitted to white-only hospitals and either died at home or in their own restricted hospitals. Indeed, it would not be until the middle of the next century that a concerted effort was made to end the segregation which was a lingering vestige of slavery.

# 6

# THE AGE OF SOCIAL REFORM

**Human Rights and Social Reform**. Many nineteenth-century intellectuals ignored or even rejected the idea of human rights derived from natural law. The intellectual climate of this period was such that those who devised important theories based them on the empirical facts they observed and on their study of history rather than on any abstract concept such as natural law. However, despite the unpopularity of human rights theories, during much of the nineteenth century many reforms were carried out which went a long way toward enhancing the human dignity of the great mass of the population. In such areas as feminism, factory legislation, trade unionism, popular education, and electoral reform, great strides were made.

The Industrial Revolution provided the impetus for this Age of Social Reform. The factory system prompted mass migration to the cities. Here the emerging working class had to face the pitiless self-interest of their employers. This situation forced workers to organize and agitate for the social reforms that were necessary for survival. It is clear that in the machine age they would not be readily granted the respect due to them as human beings unless they asserted their self-interest.

**The Chartist Movement**. When we consider that the Industrial Revolution began in Great Britain, it is not surprising that the Chartist Movement, the first organized opposition to the social order created by capitalist industry, took place there. The origin of the Chartist Movement can be traced to 1831-1832 when urban workers took part in the campaign for an electoral Reform Bill only to discover that the measure held nothing for the lower classes. In fact, the Reform Bill of 1832 had an antidemocratic tendency since it rallied the upper-middle class in Britain to support the existing order. In 1836, an association was formed which drew up a charter of demands for the urban proletariat which was presented to Parliament. The Charter *(see Reading No. 20)* demanded universal suffrage, secret ballot, salaries for members of Parliament, and annual elections. On July 12, 1839, the petition was rejected by Parliament by a vote of 235 to 46.

After this defeat, the Chartist Movement lingered on for another decade. In the revolutionary year of 1848, there was a final flare-up of Chartism which was suppressed by the police. Eventually, much of the support for the Chartist Movement was channeled into the growing Trade Union Movement and agitation for industrial reform.

**Factory Legislation.** The working conditions which prevailed in early nineteenth-century industry were appalling and dehumanizing. The worst victims were usually children whose small size and nimble fingers made them very useful for work in the mines and textile mills. They often worked six hours a day at heavy labor which permanently impaired their health. In Britain, various Parliamentary investigating commissions and reports documented these conditions. As a result, the Factory Act of 1833 was passed. This law which was applicable to most textile mills forbade the employment of anyone under nine years of age and limited the employment of older children. The Factory Act of 1844 prohibited the employment of women and children under ten in coal mines.

In France a factory law was passed in 1841 which limited the employment of children. But, unlike the British law, there was no provision for the appointment of factory inspectors so that the law was frequently evaded. Various German states, such as Bavaria and Baden, also passed factory laws. In Prussia, a factory law was passed in 1853 which stipulated that the minimum age for work in factories and mines would be gradually raised to twelve. Though one of the best laws in any industrial country, it was still very primitive.

**Popular Education.**    Nineteenth-century liberals considered themselves heirs of the Enlightenment. As such they were eager for the masses to acquire an education so that they could become enlightened, decent, and liberal. Literacy was necessary so that the masses could participate intelligently in governments which were becoming increasingly democratic. Even more importantly, literacy was necessary so that the masses would make more useful recruits for the army and more efficient workers for industry.

The first areas of Western civilization where almost everyone was literate were Prussia and the adjacent German and Scandinavian states. The impetus for popular education in this region came from rulers and clergy who wanted to produce soldiers and subjects who were obedient, disciplined, and pious. But the rest of Western civilization was far behind. In 1850, even in Great Britain and the United States, a large part of the population was illiterate.

Beginning in the late 1860s, there was a rapid growth in popular education. Industrialization was one of the major factors contributing to the increased emphasis on literacy. In the United States, the period after the Civil War witnessed a great expansion of educational institutions. Between 1870 and 1900 the school population doubled to a total of 15,000,000. There was a particularly large growth in the number of high schools which rose from 500 to 6,000. In the field of higher education, the United States was a leader. The Morrill Act of 1862 had provided subsidies to the states for the formation of colleges that were intended primarily for instruction in "agriculture and the mechanical arts." Sixty-nine colleges were set up in the post-Civil War period under this act.

In much of Europe, there was a similar expansion of popular education. In Great Britain in 1870, Gladstone's Liberal ministry increased state subsidies for denomination schools. In 1880, school attendance was made compulsory for British children. Between 1870 and 1900 the percentage of literacy rose in Great Britain from 66 percent to 95 percent. Under the Education Act of 1902 there was a further increase in government support of the school system. Such countries as France, Switzerland, Italy, and Austria-Hungary greatly increased their public education systems and passed laws requiring compulsory education. However, in Italy and Austria-Hungary where the pace of industrialization was slow, laws mandating school attendance were frequently neglected.

**Feminism.** During the era of the eighteenth-century Enlightenment little was done to further the rights of women. Even at the height of the French Revolution, women were excluded not only from the franchise but from most public meetings and political agitation. Mary Wollstonecraft's (1759-1797) *A Vindication of the Rights of Women* written in 1792 *(see Reading No. 21)* found no substantial support. In the eyes of the law women were little more than serfs or chattels.

In the nineteenth century there was a greater acceptance of the idea that women have the same human rights as men. In 1869, John Stuart Mill's *The Subjection of Women (see Reading No. 22)* found wide acceptance. Even more than other nineteenth-century reforms, the improved status of women can be related directly to increased industrialization and urbanization. The invention of the typewriter, cash register, adding machine, and telephone created numerous sedentary clerical positions which were believed to be ideally suited for women. With large numbers of women in the work force, it was inevitable that greater attention would be given to respect for their basic rights.

The right of women to their own property and their own earnings was recognized in Great Britain by Parliamentary acts in 1870 and 1882. Most other countries passed similar legislation at about the same time. There were also vastly increased opportunities for women in higher education. The University of Zurich led the way in 1867 followed shortly thereafter by universities in France, Scandinavia, Britain, and even Russia, Italy, and Greece. Small numbers of women were also allowed to practice as doctors. By 1890 women could be admitted to the medical profession in England, Holland, Belgium, Russia, and various American states. Admission of women to the legal profession, however, was not allowed until the next century.

One of the most important and persistent demands of late nineteenth-century feminists was for equal voting rights with men. In the 1870s, the suffrage movement began gaining momentum in Great Britain. In 1888 the "International Women's Suffrage Alliance" was formed whose conventions were attended by delegates from an ever-increasing number of countries. One of the first areas in the world to grant women suffrage was the western portion of the United States. Wyoming in 1869, Colorado in 1893, and Utah and Idaho in 1896 granted equal voting rights. New Zealand and portions of Australia also granted female suffrage in the 1890s. In Europe, Sweden and Finland led the way in the first decade of the twentieth century. However, it was not until after World War I that female suffrage became the accepted pattern in Western civilization.

**Trade Unionism.** The working class's main defense against dehumanization in the industrial age came from the Trade Union movement. In most countries the Trade Union movement was opposed not only by capitalists but also by government. There was usually a violent struggle before the Trade Unions were recognized. Not until 1876 in Britain, 1884 in France, and 1914 in the United States were Trade Unions fully legalized. Besides engaging in strikes for higher pay and better working conditions, early Trade Unions also administered mutual insurance funds against sickness, accident, and death. In an era before social security and the welfare state, these union insurance funds were an important protection for the working man.

In the late nineteenth-century Europe there were divergent forms of Trade Unionism. Some were nonideological trade unions which did not advocate any particular philosophy or change in the form of government. These were usually associated with or supported by progressive and liberal political parties. In the prosperous period 1886 to 1892, socialist unions sprang up in many countries. These unions sought working-class organization by industries rather than by crafts. They enlisted unskilled laborers as well as skilled artisans and were distinctly militant. They believed that the only way to further the rights of workers was to carry on a class struggle between capital and labor. The period also witnessed the emergence of Catholic trade unions in such countries as Germany, Italy, Austria, and Belgium.

In the United States trade unions made very slow progress. The first serious effort to organize a nationwide organization was the National Labor Union which was founded after the Civl War. Its demands included an eight-hour day, currency revision, restriction of immigration, and establishment of a federal Department of Labor. The National Labor Union relied more on political than economic action to better the conditions of working people. It paid little attention to collective bargaining, union recognition, and strikes. This approach proved unsuccessful and the Union soon folded.

Another attempt to found a nationwide labor movement was made by the Knights of Labor. *(See Reading No. 23.)* It represented all workers both skilled and unskilled. It rapidly grew in strength but after a series of unsuccessful strikes its membership rapidly declined. It was crushed by the aggressive tactics of the employers who did not hesitate to use violence and blacklisting against union members. A major handicap was the system of organizing both skilled and unskilled laborers in the same union. The unskilled proved to be a drag on the skilled workers who had some bargaining power.

It was not until the formation of the American Federation of Labor under Samuel Gompers (1850-1924) in 1886 that a strong union was formed in the United States. Gompers avoided politics and utopian ideals and concentrated on practical issues of higher wages and better working conditions. The A.F.L. contained only skilled workers who had some bargaining power. It was not until well into the twentieth century that unskilled workers could be organized in America. The constant waves of immigrants provided the employers with an unlimited supply of strike breakers which was a great hindrance to the development of trade unionism in the United States.

**Socialism.** One of the most significant events of the nineteenth-century was the development of Socialism. Though the pioneers of Socialist thought had little influence in their own time, they were responsible for the Socialist movements which are important in many countries in the twentieth century. At the heart of Socialist thought was a concern for the economic and social rights of the underprivileged elements which were so numerous in the developing capitalist societies. As an early advocate of French Socialism, Comte de Saint-Simon (1760-1825) stated: "The whole of society ought to strive toward the amelioration of the moral and physical existence of the poorest class; society ought to organize itself in the best way adapted for attaining this end." At a very early period, Saint-Simon advocated state interference in the economy for the benefit of workers who would be exploited in the coming industrial age. He was also a proponent of private cooperatives which would be financed by individual inheritances which would be confiscated by the state.

In England Robert Owen (1771-1858), a British mill owner, was one of the earliest Socialists. He believed that the heads of industrial enterprises were the best fitted to bring about a new spiritual direction of society which would not only create social justice but would even abolish war. Owen set up cooperative communities in which, under careful supervision, families could share in work and the enjoyment of its products. Owen based his project on the belief in the innate goodness and perfectability of mankind. The appeal was to awaken the conscience of the upper classes rather than to the workers themselves. The cooperative movement which was advocated by the moderate Socialists still survives in many countries which continue to have cooperatives for the production and distribution of various commodities.

**Marxism.** Alongside the temperate, moderate reformers, a new, more strident, "scientific socialism" was being developed by Karl Marx (1818-1883) and Friedrich Engles (1820-1895). A serious student of history and economics, Marx believed that all history is a reflection of a class struggle—in ancient Rome a struggle between patrician and plebian, in the Middle Ages a struggle between lord and peasant, and in the nineteenth-century a struggle between employer and worker. This latter struggle would inevitably result in the victory of the proletariat over the capitalist bourgeoisie and the creation of a classless socieity in which the rights of all would be secure. In 1848, Marx and Engles wrote the *Communist Manifesto* which sought to win over the working class to the idea of revolution to overthrow the capitalist system. The *Manifesto* ends with the stirring words: "The proletariat have nothing to lose but their chains. They have a world to win. Workingmen of all countries unite." In 1867, Marx published the first volume of his monumental work, *Das Kapital,* as a contribution to the education of the workers.

Marxism has had a profound influence on the modern world despite the fact that most of the Marxist predictions have been proven to be wrong. Under the capitalist system the standard of living of the working class has risen and not fallen as Marx had postulated as inevitable. The political rights of the working class have also become more secure so that there is a greater degree of freedom for all classes under capitalism than was imagined in the nineteenth century. But in those countries where Marxism has the greatest influence, human rights—political, civil, social, and economic—have not been secure.

# 7

# TOTALITARIANISM

**Definition of Totalitarianism.** After World War I, movements developed in several European countries which represented an enormous step backward in the struggle for human freedom. These totalitarian regimes combined the mass means of communication and the central bureaucracy of the modern state with the absolute discipline of the nation-at-arms and the fanaticism of twentieth-century ideology carried to its illogical extreme. Totalitarian regimes differed from conventional dictatorships in that they generally encouraged mass participation which serves as the chief basis of their power. Central to any totalitarian regime is a charismatic leader who creates about himself a "cult of personality." Also characteristic of totalitarianism is the complete subordination of the individual to the interest of the state which usually means to the interest of the totalitarian leader.

Although there is usually a hollow shell of constitutional procedure under a totalitarian regime, the civil and political rights which have been developed over several centuries are routinely ignored. Elections, when held, are merely plebiscites which retroactively endorse the decisions of the absolute leader. The press is always rigidly controlled and freedom of individual expression is non-existent. Under such a system there is a conscious effort to control the thinking of any intellectual who might dare to criticize the party line. Clearly the greatest danger to a totalitarian regime is a person with a questioning mind who shows the slightest inclination to point out that the "Emperor has no clothes." Totalitarian regimes generally fear rationality and prefer strong appeals to the emotions.

**The Totalitarian Regimes.** There is certainly room for legitimate disagreement as to which states have been genuinely totalitarian. It was Benito Mussolini who first coined the word "totalitarian" to refer to his own regime.

*(See Reading No. 24.)* However, most observers believe that Fascist Italy did not exhibit totalitarian characteristics to the same degree as Hitler's Germany or Stalinist Russia. China under Mao Tse-tung also showed strong tendencies toward totalitarianism. In all of these regimes, with varying degrees of success, an effort was made to control every aspect of human existence which was accompanied by a complete disregard for the rights and liberties of individuals. In these countries each person was seen as a cog in a wheel who was completely expendable to achieve the ideological goals of the totalitarian dictator. In our analysis of totalitarianism we shall concentrate on the regimes of Hitler, Mussolini, Mao, and Stalin, but it should be recognized that other governments in our century have exhibited totalitarian tendencies which threatened human rights.

**The Charismatic Leader.** Totalitarian dictators create about themselves a cult of personality which places them above any possible reproach from their followers. The Nazis preached the doctrine of the *"Fuehrerprinzip"* *(see Reading No. 25)* which made Adolf Hitler the absolute leader of the Nazi movement and the state. After the Nazis seized power in 1933, public officials and members of the military pledged their loyalty not to the nation but to the *Fuehrer* personally. Every German home was expected to have a portrait of Hitler and a copy of his book *Mein Kampf* which was venerated as a sacred text. It was universally understood that the fate of Germany was subordinated to Hitler's whim. The Nazi legal expert, Hans Frank (1900-1946), stated: "Our Constitution is the Will of the *Fuehrer.*" Another member of the Nazi hierarchy, Hermann Goering (1893-1946), stated: "When a decision has to be taken none of us counts more than the stones on which we are standing. It is the *Fuehrer* alone who decides."

There was also a cult of personality surrounding Stalin. When he first assumed power in the 1920s, Stalin tended not to attract a great deal of attention to himself. Gradually, a cult of personality was built up around the Soviet dictator. Eventually, numerous books, poems, and other works of art were dedicated to Comrade Stalin. The city of Tsaritsina was renamed Stalingrad in his honor while he was still alive. It was even suggested by overzealous sycophants that the Volga River and even the moon should be renamed after him! Everyone in the Soviet Union realized that Stalin had more power over them than any of the "autocratic" Czars.

A natural outgrowth of Fascist Italy's authoritarian philosophy was the cult of the *Duce*. Mussolini was venerated as if he were a superhuman figure who was all-knowing and all powerful. "The *Duce* is always right" became the password which loyal Fascists painted on walls all over the country. The deference shown to Mussolini surpassed the reverence which had been given to diven-right monarchs. All newspapers were obliged to give a prominent place to his articles and speeches. Typesetters had to print the word *DUCE* in captial letters. In the 1930s, the cinema and radio became useful vehicles for the dissemination of the *Duce* myth. Films which showed the supreme leader in various heroic poses became compulsory in every movie theater in Italy. Mussolini's voice became the most common sound on Italian state radio.

Mao Tse-tung held a position which was comparable to the other totalitarian leaders. The little red book, *The Thoughts of Chairman Mao*, was venerated in Communist China as if it were a text of sacred scripture. The cult of personality reached bizarre proportions. The portrait of Chairman Mao was seen everywhere and his speeches were quoted insistently. A myth was built up around the long years of Mao's struggle for power. This legend was used to show Chairman Mao's superhuman qualities of tenacity and wisdom.

**Civil and Political Rights Under Totalitarianism.** In all totalitarian countries no political opposition is ever tolerated. The right of any individual to express a contrary point of view is drastically curtailed. Newspapers express only the party line. Public protests against government policy are strictly forbidden. Opposition cliques within the ruling elite sometimes develop but they are quickly purged by the totalitarian leader. Despite occasional friction there is usually a close relationship between the government and the party. This intertwining of party and state prevents the party from developing into a focal point of opposition to totalitarian government policies. The destruction of civil and political rights was very apparent in the totalitarian dictatorship of Hitler and Stalin.

In Germany, Hitler destroyed the civil rights which had been enjoyed under the former Weimar constitution. Shortly after the Nazis took power, an emergency presidential decree for the "Protection of the People and State" was passed. It suspended all civil rights thus permitting the *Fuehrer* to rule by a sort of continual martial law. Hitler destroyed the rule of law which had traditionally existed in Germany. Under such leaders as Frederick the Great (1712-1786), Bismarck (1815-1898), and Kaiser Wilhelm II (1859-1941), Germans had been proud that they lived under the *"Rechsttatt" i.e.,* a country which was goverend by the rule of law which even the head of state could not violate. But under the Nazis there were no longer even the theoretical guarantees of legal protection for basic civil rights.

In Stalin's Russia there was an effort to pretend that the basic civil liberties were guaranteed. In 1936, Stalin promulgated a constitution which was designed to fit the reality of a strong authoritarian tightly centralized one-party state. Under Stalin's constitution, all citizens had equal rights regardless of their nationality, race, or sex. All citizens were guaranteed freedom of conscience and the right to work, recreation, and education. The Stalin constitution also guaranteed freedom of speech, press, assembly, and association, the inviolability of person and domicile, as well as secrecy of the mail. However, the operative clause states that these rights could be disregarded "in the interest of strengthening the Socialist society." In point of fact, all human rights were violated with impunity in Stalin's Russia without regard to the constitution or any other written guarantee.

**Freedom of Religion.** Because totalitarian leaders create about themselves a semireligious cult, they tend to be intolerant of established religion. It is considered dangerous for anyone to have any loyalty outside the system. The sense of morality which is taught by most religions represents a possible source of conflict in a totalitarian system. If the leader is always right, his decisions cannot be subject to the moral review of religious leaders who could serve as organizers of an opposition movement. Most totalitarian regimes have made an effort to control religion and, if possible, use it to bolster the system. Some religious leaders have collaborated with totalitarian regimes but many have suffered because of their independence and resistance.

In Germany, the Nazis had little respect for Christianity. Their real preference was for a revival of the Old Teutonic worship in which glorification of war, racial intolerance, and blind obedience to authority would replace the Christian teachings of love, brotherhood, and respect for human dignity. To the Nazis, the Catholic Church was particularly suspect because it had ties to an international hierarchy outside the country. They resented the idea of separate Catholic schools in which the youth would not receive the necessary Nazi indoctrination. Catholic clergy who spoke up for freedom of conscience were quickly silenced by the Nazis. Not a few Catholic clergy ended up in concentration camps.

Hitler also sought to control the Protestant churches. The Nazis set up a Reich Church which taught a new form of German Christianity. Bishop Mueller, a friend of Hitler, was appointed as its head. This church preached doctrines which followed the Nazi line. Some extreme "German Christians" wished to eliminate the *Old Testament,* exclude all converted Jews, and require that all pastors take an oath of allegiance to the *Fuehrer.* Such "reforms" would have destroyed the autonomy and integrity of the Protestant Church in Germany.

Fortunately not all Protestant clergymen were willing to do Hitler's bidding. Many churchmen held firm to the humanistic tradition of German Protestantism. The Reverend Martin Niemoeller set up a "Confessional Church" which became the rival of the Nazi-sponsored Reich Church. Paster Niemoeller objected to the Nazi doctrine of "Race, Blood and Soil" being brought into the Church. Many Confessional pastors were arrested and their churches harassed in every possible way. Eventually, Pastor Niemoeller was sent to a concentration camp. Another martyr was Pastor Dietrich Bonhoeffer (1906-1945), who was arrested in 1942 and held for two and a half years without trial. This brave exponent of human rights and personal integrity was put to death in Flossenburg concentration camp only a few days before the end of World War II.

In Fascist Italy, Mussolini could not eliminate the influence of the Vatican easily since the Catholic Church was one of the most powerful institutions in the country. In 1929 the *Duce* signed a Concordat with the Church but there were constant conflicts over the interpretation of this agreement. In 1931 a dispute arose over Catholic Action, a youth group which the Pope saw as a defense of Christian social principles. The Fascists viewed with alarm the existence of any body which impinged on the claims of the totalitarian state. After considerable tension, the Church was forced to accept a limitation on the activities of Catholic Action. Whenever possible the *Duce* used the prestige of the Church to bolster his own regime. There were, however, individual clerics who refused to cooperate with Fascism despite the pro-Catholic statements of many Fascist leaders.

The Communist ideology is hostile to religion which Marx saw as the opium of the people. Under Stalin freedom of religion was nonexistent. Churches were often attacked, pillaged, and forced to close. Many churches were "voluntarily" turned into museums of atheism. Schools preached antireligious propaganda. The League of Militant Atheists was active throughout the country particularly among the youth. Many clergymen were sent to labor camps. Those who were suspected of favoring religion were in constant fear of being denounced as "counterrevolutionaries."

**Cultural Freedom.** In the effort to control every aspect of human existence, totalitarian regimes invariably make an effort to limit the cultural expressions of the people under their control. A good example of this was the suppression of culture which took place in Nazi Germany. Nazism represented a total rejection of the humanistic cultural tradition which had developed in Western Europe to which Germany had made a major contribution. The Nazis burned huge piles of books including the works of Sigmund Freud, Erich Maria Remarque, Heinrich Heine, Thomas Mann, and Stefan Zweig. Reich Chambers of Culture were set up to control various aspects of Germany's cultural life. A Chamber of Culture could expel or refuse to accept members who were considered politically "unreliable." Such people would be excluded from practicing their profession and thus were deprived of their livelihood. Almost all of Germany's leading writers left the country. The president of the Reich Theatre Chamber boasted publicly that whenever someone mentioned the word "culture," he wanted to reach for his revolver.

In the field of painting, Hitler personally burned works which he disapproved of since he considered himself an art expert. Paintings by Picasso, Van Gogh, Gauguin, Matisse, and Cezanne were removed from German museums. In 1937, Hitler inaugurated the "House of German Art" in Munich which displayed examples of sterile, tasteless Nazi art. As in other fields, German artists with an urge to create original and imaginative work had to leave Germany.

The Nazis were particularly severe in their censorship of press, radio, and films. Dr. Joseph Goebbels, the Nazi

Propaganda Minister, gave out daily directives on what the newspapers should write and what should be broadcast over the radio. The right of the public to have access to objective and comprehensive information was totally ignored. As in all totalitarian societies, the population was fed a steady diet of propaganda. Goebbels, like Hitler, believed in the "big lie" — if a lie, no matter how preposterous, is repeated often enough, it would be accepted as the truth. In Nazi Germany, there was no opportunity for the public to make intelligent decisions of their own on key issues. All newspapers, magazines, radio programs, and films repeated only one perspective—the Nazi party line. Eventually, the number of newspaper readers declined since there was no need for the public to consult more than one publication for they all contained the same story.

The area where German culture had made the greatest contribution was in the physical sciences. In many fields of science Germany had been preeminent. But the Nazis feared the spirit of free inquiry and rationality which is the basis of all science. Scientists had to conform to Nazi theories or, like other intellectuals, were forced to emigrate. Many who were of Jewish origin, such as Albert Einstein, Max Born, and James Franck, left Germany and made major contributions to countries which opposed Nazism.

Another totalitarian country where the suppression of free inquiry was counterproductive was Maoist China during the Cultural Revolution. In 1966, China underwent a huge domestic upheaval, the aim of which was a total revamping of Chinese society which would eliminate the "four 'olds'—old habits, manners, customs, and culture." Maoist radicals believed they could achieve a shortcut to utopian Communism by ignoring a rational evaluation of the Chinese situation and replacing it with a blind belief in doctrine and reliance on force and the power of human will. The educational system of the country was disrupted as hordes of students left school to become Red Guards— the young cadres who would carry the Cultural Revolution all over China. The young people of the country were easily caught up in this phenomenon since it put them at the center of national life and offered them free trips to Peking and other prerequisities.

Thousands of highly skilled intellectuals were purged from Chinese life. In the field of science, valuable work on cancer research was halted since many of the leading specialists were forced by radicals who believed that fanatic devotion to Chairman Mao was more important than technical proficiency. In one extreme case, Chinese newspapers carried the story of a young man who fought off a malignant tumor without medical treatment because he was "imbued with Mao Tse-tung's thought." The Red Guards were highly suspicious of Western medicine which was based on the scientific method of free inquiry which they distrusted.

A favorite tactic of the Red Guards was the use of wall posters which attacked leading figures in a variety of fields—literature, music, motion pictures, and the fine arts. Many of these intellectuals were sent for "study training" at Socialist Institutes which amounted to concentration camps for prominent cultural figures. There these unfortunate people were organized into brigades supervised by army officers. The intellectuals were required to read Maoist literature and participate in endless meetings where they were encouraged to denounce themselves and each other.

Many intellectuals were forced to clean latrines and perform a considerable amount of strenuous and pointless physical labor. The Red Guards frequently attacked and beat these culturally prominent people, many of whom were their former professors. The conditions which prevailed in Maoist China during the Cultural Revolution give a good indication of the precarious position of free thought in a totalitarian regime.

**Definition of Genocide**. Related to totalitarianism and often its direct consequence is the policy of persecution and mass murder which as come to be known as genocide. The word "genocide" was coined in 1944 by Raphael Lemkin to describe the actions carried out by the Nazis and Italian Fascists in the countries which they occupied during World War II. The concept was later used as the basis for the Genocide Convention which was approved by the United Nations General Assembly on December 9, 1948 *(See Reading No. 26.)* For technical reasons the General Assembly did not mention political groups in the list of those to be protected by the Convention. However, many authorities support a broader definition of genocide which would include the persecution of any group "on grounds of national or racial origin, religious belief or political opinion of its members." For our purposes, we shall consider those cases of twentieth-centry genocide which are covered by this definition.

Of course, examples of genocide can be found throughout recorded history. The extermination of many American Indian tribes is a notable example. However, the mass means of communication, greater organizational development, and ideological fanaticism common in the twentieth century have accentuated man's age-old tendencay to exterminate his neighbors. Genocide has been and remains one of the greatest threats to human rights.

**The Armenian Massacres**. Wartime conditions can often produce the isolation from outside interference which is necessary for genocide. This occurred during World War I, when the Turks massacred a large part of the Armenians living under their rule. For centuries the Chirstian Armenians had suffered at the hands of the Turks. In the late nineteenth century, the Turks intensified their oppression as a reaction against Armenian agitation for independence. In 1896, under Sultan Abdul

Hamid there were widespread massacres. In 1908, the Young Turk movement overthrew the Sultan and formed a democratic government which at first had a more humane attitude toward the Armenian minority.

However, after Turkey entered World War I on the side of the Central Powers, there was a renewed and greatly intensified persecution of the Armenians. Cut off from the outside world, the Turks used the opportunity to begin an organized and systematic annihilation of the Armenian people. First of all, the adult males were arrested, taken away, and killed. Then the women and children were forced out of their homes and driven into the mountains and deserts to die of starvation and exposure. Out of 3 million Armenians living within the boundaries of Turkey, 2 million died and the rest were dispersed.

**Early Soviet Genocide.** During most of World War I, Bolshevik revolutionaries favored separatist movement activities among many national groups in the Russian Empire. Indeed, soon after seizing power, the Bolsheviks issued a declaration of rights for the peoples of Russia. But this policy quickly changed. In 1922, Lenin denounced the right of minorities to national independence. The Bolsheviks strove to reestablish the Empire in the form of a highly centralized Soviet state. The cultural, religious, linguistic, and racial diversity of the country was seen as a threat to the new regime. Ethnic groups which resisted the Soviet system were treated with increasing harshness. Many groups were not only denied the right of self-determination but were the victims of a brutal campaign of extermination.

One of the most unfortunate early cases of Soviet genocide was the campaign against the Crimean Tartars. After the Bolsheviks occupied the Crimea in November 1920, power was given to the notorious Hungarian Communist, Bela Kun (1885-1937). Because he believed that the Tartars were unreliable, Bela Kun sought to eliminate them. In the first phase of the terror, 70,000 people were executed without trial or judicial proceedings. Then, in the winter of 1921-1922, a terrible famine gripped the region. This was purposely manipulated by the Bolsheviks who had exported a large part of the year's harvest from the Crimea. Foodstuff sent to the area by the Internatinal Red Cross was seized by the Bolsheviks who wished to see the Crimean Tartars annihilated. As a result of this policy, 100,000 people died unnecessarily of starvation in the Crimea. The decimation of the Crimean Tartars and the other atrocities committed under Lenin were certainly gruesome but were overshadowed by the terror perpetrated by his successor, Joseph Stalin.

**Soviet Genocide Under Stalin.** For Stalin, genocide was a tool of state policy which he used in order to eliminate national, religious, racial, and political groups. Estimates of the total number of people exterminated during his reign run as high as 20 or 30 million. Most of his victims had never committed a single act of opposition to the regime. All that was necessary to incur the dictator's wrath was for an individual or group to possess the potential for resistance. This alone was enough to invite disaster in Stalinist Russia. After the dictator's death, his successors denounced his crimes. *(See Reading No. 27.)* But even today the full extent of Stalin's genocidal excesses are hardly known by the present generation in the Soviet Union.

**The Horrors of Collectivization.** One of the greatest impediments to the achievement of an equitable standard of human rights in many countries is the animosity which exists between various social classes. This friction can often erupt into violence and can sometimes lead to social genocide. Perhaps the worst example of social genocide occurred in the Soviet Union between 1927 and 1933 when Stalin attempted the collectivization of Soviet argriculture. Stalin was anxious to collectivize Soviet argriculture out of the holdings of small independent landowners whom he hoped to eliminate. Not unexpectedly, collectivization was not accepted willingly. It had to be imposed by the state with overwhelming violence.

In 1932-1933, an artificially created famine gripped the agricultural regions of the country. Many peasants were sent to labor camps when they refused to relinquish their right to the land which they had worked on for generations. Crops were seized and the specter of starvation fell over the rich agricultural areas of the Ukraine, North Caucasus, and the Don basin. Meanwhile, the Soviet government exported huge quantities of grain to foreign countries at prices which barely covered the cost of freight. Perhaps as many as 6 million died of starvation and disease caused by hunger. Another 3 million were sent to labor camps, few of whom survived. This was the price of collectivization.

**The Great Terror.** Unfortunately, the horrors of collectivization were only the beginning of the tortures which Stalin was to inflict on the people of his country. On December 1, 1934, the Leningrad Party Secretary Sergei Kirov was assassinated. Many people believe that Stalin had ordered the murder in order to justify the wave of mass terror which soon swept over the country. Millions were arrested, most of whom were executed or sent to forced labor camps. This included scientists, diplomats, government officials, army officers, intellectuals, and most of the early leaders of the Bolshevik Revolution. A semblance of legality and judicial procedure was used to conduct this great purge. Many were sentenced under Article 58 of the Criminal Code (which covered "political" offenses). However, such legislation which inflicted penalties on the families of "traitors" who fled abroad represented an enormous step backward in the protection of human rights. The purge in the 1930s was a form of social genocide aimed against members of the strata of society which had the potential (but not necessarily the desire) to resist Stalin's rule. Perhaps because he feared betrayal in the anticipated war with Nazi Germany, and out of an extreme paranoia, the Soviet dictator wished to rid himself of those elements in society which could overthrow his rule in a moment of crisis.

During World War II, any ethnic group which was suspected of disloyalty was shipped to labor camps en masse. Stalin sent the Kalmyks, Ingush, Balkar, Chechen, Volga

Germans, Karachai, and the remnants of the Crimean Tartars to Siberia because he believed they were capable of collaborating with the Nazi invaders. One of the greatest tragedies of World War II was the fate of Soviet prisoners of war who returned to their country. Because they had surrendered to the Nazis, Stalin suspected them of disloyalty. After years of brutal Nazi captivity, these men were arrested on their return home and shipped to Soviet labor camps.

**Stalin's Gulags.** Conditions in Soviet labor camps during the Stalin era have no parallel in Russian history. The Siberian exile imposed by the Czars was miniscule in scale and conditions were luxurious in comparison to life in a Soviet labor camp. These institutions served a double purpose of eliminating the social classes and ethnic groups which were considered undesirable as well as providing slave labor to perform the work that could not otherwise be undertaken. In view of the endless toil, inadequate food, shelter, and clothing in the near-Arctic climate, there was a constant turnover of inmates. In many camps special teams were assigned to pick up the frozen bodies after each work detail was completed.

The inmates in the camps were constantly terrorized by sadistic guards, trustees, and common criminals who served as a camp aristocracy. Many people suffered and died in the camps without ever knowing why they were there. Perhaps the greatest tragedy of Stalin's Gulags was that for many of them there really was no reason.

**Mussolini's Policy of Genocide.** The word genocide very accurately describes the brutal Italian Fascist occupation policy in the Balkans during World War II. It could also be used to describe Mussolini's policy in Italy's African colonies. As early as 1930, Mussolini carried on an extermination campaign in Libya against the Senussi religious sect. Tens of thousands died in concentration camps, terror raids, and en route to forced exile in Egypt. Somewhat later, in 1935-1936, the Italian Fascists launched their genocidal war and occupation of Ethiopia. Many "battles" in this conflict resembled hunting expeditions in which nearly defenseless Ethiopian hordes were bombed and inundated with poison gas. During the occupation of the country, entire districts were virtually depopulated by the Fascist invaders. In all 700,000 Ethiopians died during the Italian occupation, most of whom were defenseless noncombatants.

During World War II, Mussolini occupied Albania and parts of Greece and Yugoslavia. His forces were responsible for the death of hundreds of thousands of people in concentration camps, manipulated famines, and in terror raids on defenseless villages. In Yugoslavia, there was a concerted effort to wipe out the Croatian people who lived along the Dalmatian Coast. Over 200 Italian concentration camps were set up in Yugoslavia in which hundreds of thousands of people suffered severe privation. As in other areas the ultimate goal of Italian Fascist genocide was to eliminate the local population so that the region could be settled with colonists from Italy.

**Nazi Racial Theory.**   Perhaps the most infamous example of the use of genocide as state policy occurred in Nazi Germany. Long before he came to power, Adolf Hitler wrote in *Mein Kampf* expounding his theory that the German people were a superior Aryan race destined to dominate and to exterminate inferior nations and ethnic groups. *(See Reading No. 28.)* Hitler believed that it was necessary for the German people to eliminate Jews and other alien elements within their midst and then to acquire living space for the Aryan race by conquering the Slavic-inhabited regions of Eastern Europe.

At the heart of Nazi racism was a complete unashamed denial of Western civilization's concept of human rights. The very humanity of Jews, Gypsies, and Slavs was denied, thus making these groups eligible for mass extermination. The genocidal policy initiated by Nazi Germany was the most disturbing violation of human rights to be carried out in our century.

**Hitler's Extermination of Jews.**   The principal target of Hitler's insane genocidal policy was the Jews. Soon after he came to power, the *Fuehrer* began taking measures against Germany's Jewish population. On September 15, 1935, the Nuremberg Laws were unanimously adopted in the *Reichstag.* Marriage and extra-marital sex between Jews and German "Aryans" were forbidden. Jews were denied all of their rights as German citizens. After these preliminary measures were taken, the Nazis wavered as to what should be done with Germany's Jewish population. Some of Hitler's advisers favored a policy of forced migration. Other Nazi leaders such as the Propaganda Minister Paul Josef Goebbels proposed that the Jews should be confined to formalized ghettos similar to what had existed in the Middle Ages.

On January 30, 1939, Hitler stated: "If international finance Jewry . . . should succeed once more in plunging the peoples into a world war then the consequence will be . . . the destruction of the Jewish race in Europe." During World War II, the Nazis took steps to implement this threat. On January 20, 1942, at the Wannsee Conference, leaders of the Third Reich met to coordinate policy for the Final Solution of the Jewish question. Plans were made to seize control of the Jews in as many European countries as possible. It was hoped that all of European Jewry could be "evacuated to the East," which was the euphemism for mass slaughter.

During the latter part of the war six million Jews were killed, mostly in Eastern Europe. In the early stages many died in mobile gas vans and in mass shootings. Gradually, at Auschwitz and other death camps, a system was organized in which people were gassed and their remains were cremated.

**The Gypsies.** The Jews, however, were not the only ethnic group persecuted by the Nazis. The Nazis maintained that the Gypsies were not Europeans despite the fact that they had lived there for many centuries. According to "racial scientists," the Gypsies were an alien race who were asocial, immoral, criminal, lazy, and uneducatable, and thus worthy candidates for elimination. In 1938, the Nazis passed a law entitled "The Fight against the Gypsy Menace." The purpose of the law was to find and identify all Gypsies on German and Austrian soil by forcing them to register with the police. In 1940, all Gypsies in the German Reich were deported to Nazi occupied Poland. The actual extermination of Gypsies began in 1942. As with the massacre of the Jews, many Fascist groups in Eastern Europe collaborated with the Germans in their genocidal campaign against the Gypsies. In Yugoslavia, the pro-Fascist Ustashi murdered tens of thousands of Gypsies. In all, perhaps as many as half a million Gypsies were murdered by the Nazis and their allies.

**The Slavs.** The largest group targeted for Nazi genocide were the Slavic peoples of Eastern Europe especially the Poles, the Ukrainians, and the Russians. In *Mein Kampf,* Hitler had written: "Slavs are a mass of born slaves." After the conquest of Poland in 1939, the Nazis launched an extensive campaign to terrorize local populations and prepare the country for colonization. Hitler's plan was to exterminate the intelligentsia and ruling classes in Poland and reduce the remainder of the population to serfs working for German colonists. A similar pattern emerged in the Ukraine after the Nazi invasion of the Soviet Union in June 1941. Hitler had long desired this rich agricultural region which he saw as the breadbasket for his future Teutonic Empire. The Nazi *Fuehrer* hoped to settle Eastern Europe with 20 million Germans which would necessitate a drastic reduction in the local population. Many Slavic people of Eastern Europe were transported to Nazi Germany where they were used as slave laborers for the Third Reich. These people lived under the most appalling conditions. Many of those that survived found that their health had been permanently impaired. In all, perhaps as many as 10 million defenseless Slavic people were murdered in Eastern Europe. It took many decades for this area to recover from the physical destruction and human slaughter inflicted by the Nazis.

**Recent Examples of Genocide.** The problem of genocide did not end with the demise of Hitler, Stalin, and Mussolini. In Africa there have been attempts in many countries to wipe out tribal minorities. In South America, there are continued reports of the slaughter of various Indian tribes who stand in the way of "civilization." Perhaps the worst recent example of social genocide took place in Cambodia in 1976-1978 under the extreme left-wing regime of Pol-Pot. Reports indicate that as many as two million people were slaughtered because the Communist government wished to remove all social classes that might oppose their regime. Only extreme vigilance by the international community can prevent the recurrence of similar tragedies.

# 9

# HUMAN RIGHTS IN THE CONTEMPORARY WORLD

In recent years there has been a worldwide renewed concern about the suppression of human rights. In part, this has been a reaction to the alarming increase in the violation of human rights in every section of the globe, particularly in the emerging nations of the Third World. In the early years of his administration, President Jimmy Carter announced a policy of using American influence to promote human rights around the world. *(See Reading No. 29.)* This policy was applauded by various groups for different reasons, which of course is not surprising. Those who have right-wing or conservative political views are fond of pointing out human rights violations in Communist or Marxist-oriented regimes. Liberals and those with leftist leanings criticize the human rights policies in countries ruled by reactionary military juntas which are under the influence of Western imperialism. There is, unfortunately, no lack of evidence to support the accusations of both conservatives and liberals. There are violations of human rights in countries of every political persuasion. It is, of course, impossible to describe conditions in all nations where human rights are imperiled. However, we will review the situation in Africa, Eastern Europe, Latin America, and Asia, concentrating on those countries where violations of human rights have taken place within the last few years.

## AFRICA

**Black Africa.** A large part of the African continent which was once dominated by white colonialism is now independent. The introduction of black rule has not however ended the problem of human rights violations. Most of Africa suffers from severe tribal disputes since few of the new states are ethnically homogeneous. The conflict between various tribes for control of the central government in many countries does not permit the necessary stability for the maintenance of civil and political liberties. Indeed, nearly half of Africa is ruled by authoritarian military or military-civilian coalitions. In many countries there are no traditional or indigenous institutions which can function to protect individual rights. Too often the separation of branches of government has been abandoned in favor of extraordinary powers. Many African political leaders who are unschooled in the ways of democratic institutions are overly sensitive to criticism. Citizens protesting a violation of their rights are considered as subversives threatening the existence of the state. Their criticisms are seen as an insult to the national leadership. Controversy is regarded not as a matter to be resolved by objective adjudication but as a personal challenge which is often overcome with brutal force. Most African states have one-party rule which can serve as an instrument for dictatorship. Elections have disappeared in many countries and in others are a mere formality. One of the principal threats to human rights are security forces which have almost unlimited powers. Every member of the secret police is a mobile court who often serves as instant judge, jury, and executioner.

**Uganda.** The regime of Idi Amin in Uganda is symbolic of the violation of human rights in black Africa. While in power Amin perpetrated crimes which gained him worldwide attention and a reputation as a "black Hitler." Amin seized control of Uganda in January 1971 in a military *coup d'etat*. His predecessor Milton Obote had unwittingly prepared the way for Amin's military dictatorship, In his attempt to unite a country plagued by tribal division, Obote had abolished freedom of the press, eliminated all political opposition, and instituted preventive detention. His fatal error was to expand the army which under Amin turned against him.

Once in power Amin ruled as a military dictator. He openly favored Islam and persecuted the Christian churches. Amin boasted of his admiration for Adolf Hitler. Like his Nazi mentor, he began a campaign of racial persecution which was aimed against the 75,000 Asians who played a prominent role in Uganda's economy. Amin accused the Indian and other Asian merchants of economically exploiting Uganda. He needed a scapegoat for his own economic and foreign policy failures. He also wished to confiscate Asian property so that he could reward his henchmen. On August 5, 1972, Amin announced the expulsion of the Asians from Uganda. At about the same time, he sent a letter to the Secretary-General of the United Nations praising Hitler's extermination of the Jews. Amin's persecution of the Asians not only hurt them but was also a severe blow to the Ugandan economy.

Thousands of black Ugandans suffered a fate worse than that of the Asian minority. Under Amin, executions and mass murder were commonplace. Many died while being held in prison or under detention by the army. There was an extremely gruesome aspect to Amin's atrocities. Victims were frequently dismembered. His victims were numbered in the hundreds of thousands.

Amin's crimes were so blatant and so widely publicized that he became an embarrassment to all of Africa. In April 1979, the army of Tanzania invaded Uganda and Amin was overthrown. The dictator fled into exile and is believed to be living somewhere in the Moselm world. Unfortunately, the situation in Uganda remains unstable but it is hoped that tranquility will soon return to this troubled land.

**South Africa.**   Until recently all Southern Africa was under white domination. However, with the end of white rule in Rhodesia (which became Zimbabwe in 1980) and the independence of the former Portugese colonies of Angola and Mozambique, the Union of South Africa remains the last country in Africa where blacks are excluded from the government. In South Africa, a white minority rules a highly industrialized nation of 30 million, 85 percent of which is Asian, black African, or officially classified as coloured (of mixed racial ancestry). This situation has aroused global indignation in view of the inferior political, legal, economic, and social status of the nonwhites which constitutes one of the most glaring violations of human rights in the contemporary world. Indeed, while the rest of Africa has been moving in the direction of racial equality since 1948, South Africa has been imposing its policy of racial *Apartheid* (apartness) with increasing vehemence.

**The Historical Background**. The white man came to South Africa in 1652 when the Dutch East Indies Company established an outpost in what is now Cape Town. The Dutch ruled the region until 1815 when it was ceded to England by the Congress of Vienna. The Dutch settlers did not welcome British rule, particularly the abolition of slavery in 1834. In order to escape the British, they moved north into the interior of the continent in what is known as the Great Trek. They clashed with and conquered black tribes who were moving south. Dutch settlers developed their own language and customs and came to be known as Afrikaners. They set up independent republics which they hoped would remain free of British influence. Ultimately, however, when gold and diamonds were discovered in the independent republics, they were taken over by the British after a war which ended in 1902. In 1910, the Union of South Africa was formed as an independent Dominion within the British Empire.

For many years, the Dutch-descended Afrikaners had little political influence in the country which was dominated by English-speaking South Africans. But in 1948, the Afrikaner-dominated Nationalist Party gained a majority in the House of Assembly. Within a few years they passed many of the laws which implemented the *Apartheid* program.

**The Status of Blacks in South Africa**. In every area of life in South Africa, there is a hierarchy of privilege with the whites on top, the Asian and coloured in the middle, and the African blacks on the very bottom. In housing, blacks are forced to live in townships. These are huge slums which exist outside every South African city. Whereas white South Africans enjoy one of the highest standards of living in the world, black townships are without electricity, clean water, movie theaters, or shopping areas. Africans are only allowed inside the white cities during working hours. At work they have the lowest jobs. Their right to join labor unions, to strike, or to move into more highly skilled jobs is severely limited. If we look at a recent wage scale in the mining industry, we get some idea of the economic discrimination encountered by South African blacks. White mine workers are paid an average of about $800 a month, Asians $200, coloured $170, and African blacks $40. Thus, whites earn twenty times as much as blacks who do the heaviest and most dangerous work. This is typical of South African industry.

In the area of education, the discrimination is also glaring. The government expenditure for the education of African children on a per capita basis is only one-fifteenth that for white children. Blacks go to schools in which there are few teachers, few books, and a limited curriculum. At the unversity level, despite the fact that they form the overwhelming majority of the population, blacks constitute less than 10 percent of the enrollment, mostly in correspondence courses. In view of the lack of commitment to black education, it is obvious that the government has little interest in raising the status of the black population.

Indeed, the long-range plan of the South African government calls for the creation of Bantustans which would be territorial homelands set aside as reservations for the black population. These homelands are being formed out of the least productive territory in the country. The South African Government considers the homelands as theoretically independent countries organized on a tribal basis. Eventually every South African black would be forced to become a citizen of one of the homelands even if he has lived and worked in the white portion of South Africa all his life. Blacks would be allowed to remain in townships or on farms in the white portion of the country but they would be considered citizens of their tribal homelands and thus foreigners in South Africa. This scheme would in fact make most blacks legally aliens in a land where they and their ancestors have lived and worked for generations. Relocation to the homelands would be impossible since these areas lack the industry, agriculture, or any other resource to accommodate the entire black population of South Africa. The homelands policy is being used to provide a legal fiction for the denial of rights to the blacks of South Africa. Many would become citizens of homelands which they have never seen or whose language they could not speak.

**Black Protests.** Over the past three decades the blacks of South Africa have vigorously protested the repressive policies carried out by a government in which they were not represented. In January 1952, leaders of the African National Congress demanded the abolition of discriminatory laws and direct representation for blacks in parliaments and municipal councils as their "inherent right." In June 1955, blacks along with allied Asian, coloured, and white organizations held a massive Congress of the People at Kliptown near Johannesburg in June 1955. There they adopted the Freedom Charter which formulated demands for the end of discrimination in South Africa. As the decade came to a close, militant Pan-Africanism, which was sweeping the continent, began to have an influence in South Africa. The Pan-Africanist Congress was formed in South Africa in 1959. It was this group which on March 21, 1960, organized demonstrations in Sharpsville in which sixty-seven unarmed blacks were shot down by the police. The government reaction after the incident was extremely severe. There were numerous arrests. All black protest movements were outlawed. Throughout the 1960s, black protest, at least on the surface, was successfully muted.

Beginning in 1969 with the founding of the South African Student Organization, there was a reemergence of black militancy which was led by black university students. This spirit of resistance spread to high school students. Thus, in June 1976, high school students rioted in Soweto, the black township outside Johannesburg. Since then, outbreaks led by high school students have been common in South Africa. The police react with brutality but his does not seem to have deterred the youngsters. For South Africa the future appears ominous. There are reports that 15,000 young blacks have left for guerilla training outside the country. In view of the intransigence of the white minority, blacks may well decide that a civil war is the only way for them to gain the rights which they have been denied for centuries.

## ASIA

**India.** Perhaps the best test case as to whether the civil, political, social, and economic rights of the masses can be protected in an underdeveloped country can be found in India. With most of her population illiterate, undernourished, and disease-ridden peasants, it is not easy to see how a society which is always on the brink of disaster can provide for the human rights needs of its citizens. The temptation is alwasy great for any impoverished Third World country to attempt to solve its problems more rapidly with some type of authoritarian regime which will sacrifice human rights in order to achieve economic progress. As the world's largest democracy, India's decisions will have an enormous effect on the status of human rights in the Third World.

**Indira Gandhi.** From national independence until his death in 1964, India was ruled by Jawaharlal Nehru. Despite numerous difficulties, Nehru steered the country in the direction of a genuine parliamentary democracy on a West European model. In 1966, Nehru's daughter, Indira Gandhi, became Prime Minister. At first she continued her father's democratic policies. In the early 1970s however, her administration was beset with disaster. India's economic situation, which was always precarious, took a further turn for the worse. Drought, strikes, and the international conflict over Bangladesh created a crisis for India's democratic regime. In addition, Mrs. Gandhi was involved in a court case over charges of malpractice on her part during an election campaign. On June 10, 1975, the Indian High Court ruled against Mrs. Gandhi and ordered her to step down as Prime Minister. She publicly stated that she would not obey this ruling. On June 25, 1975, at her instigation, the President of India proclaimed a state of emergency. This measure ended democracy in India. During the period when the decree was in force every conceivable right of the Indian people was violated.

While the emergency lasted, the press in India was gaged. A news agency, *Samachar,* was especially created by the government to give out the official version of events. This was the only sort of news which the press was allowed to publish under Mrs. Gandhi's regime. People could be arrested and detained for any length of time without trial. The police were given powers which made them the supreme authorities in the land. An air of fear pervaded the country. Numerous arrests were made especially of opposition leaders and members of religious and ethnic protests groups. There were frequent reports of torture. The rights of workers were freely violated during the emergency. Strikes were banned in many areas of the economy. Some wages were reduced and benefits rescinded.

One of the worst violations of basic human rights was the campaign which forced hundreds of thousands of people to undergo sterilization operations. India, of course, suffers from an enormous problem of overpopulation. Many experts believe that voluntary sterilization could be a useful tool in a coordinated program of population control. However, during the period of Mrs. Gandhi's dictatorial rule, in certain parts of the country orders were given to round up every male member of a village for sterilization without regard to age, size of family, or economic circumstance. In some cases, the salaries of government employees, such as school teachers, were withheld unless they could provide evidence that they had participated in the effort to round up people for the sterilization campaign. This tragic policy convinced millions of Indian peasants that government health workers were their worst enemies. To many people, hospitals and clinics became symbols of oppression.

Many of the excesses during the emergecy were committed by Sanjay Gandhi, the Prime Minister's son. Although he held no government position, Sanjay demanded and received the respect given to very high-ranking officials. Members of the youth organization which he headed behaved with considerable arrogance. Typical of Sanjay's brutality was his "Clean Delhi" campaign. He vowed that nothing would be spared in the effort to enhance the appearance of the city of Delhi. When the residents of an unsightly shantytown refused to leave, he ordered bulldozers to level the dwellings with the people still in them. This resulted in the death of over 100 innocent people who were crushed by construction vehicles.

In January 1977, Mrs. Gandhi relaxed the state of emergency and called new elections. She was defeated and replaced by Prime Minister Movargi Desai of the Janata Party. Under his direction India returned to the path of democracy. In January 1980, after a split in the Janata Party, Mrs. Gandhi was voted back to office. There were hopes that she would respect and maintain the democratic and constitutional traditions which are the pride of India.

**South Korea.** One of the best examples of a regime which receives American aid while denying the human rights of its own people is South Korea. The excuse given for the suppression of human rights is the threat of Communist agression. With the Communist regime in North Korea and the lingering memory of the invasion of the early 1950s, there is obviously reason for concern. However, there can be no justification for the degree of repression which exists in South Korea. In recent years there has been considerable economic progress. However, because of the lack of basic freedoms, many educated South Koreans emigrated to the United States where they hoped to find a higher standard of human rights.

Unfortunately, it appears unlikely that those who remain in South Korea will see the end of repression in the near future. For many years, the country's large army has been the dominant influence in the political life of the country. In May 1961, General Park Chung Hee came to power after he engineered a bloodless military coup. Park was elected President in 1963 and reelected on several occasions. The South Korean Yushin constitution guarantees most basic rights; however, the President is authorized to suspend these rights in an emergency. The government of Park Chung Hee used this constitutional provision to pass laws suppressing students, clergymen, and members of the political opposition. In October 1979, President Park was assassinated. In December, General Chon Too Hwan seized control of the army. On September 1, 1980, General Chon was inaugurated as President of South Korea. President Chon called for "Korean-style democracy." This would be an authoritarian regime under a powerful executive, a weak legislature, and a judiciary chosen and controlled by the President. As with his predecessors, General Chon does not give a high priority to human rights.

## EASTERN EUROPE

Since World War II, the Soviet Union has dominated most of Eastern Europe including Poland, Bulgaria, Rumania, Czechoslovakia, Hungary, and East Germany. Yugoslavia under its leader Marshal Tito (1892-1980) successfully broke away for the Soviet bloc in 1948. Rumania exercised a great deal of independence in foreign affairs but mullified the Soviets by maintaining considerable domestic repression. In 1956, Hungary attempted to break away from the Soviet bloc and throw out the Communist rulers. This revolt was crushed by the Soviet Union in a brutal act of repression.

Under the rule of Nikita Khrushchev (1894-1971) in the late 1950s and early 1960s, there was a noticeable liberalization in the Communist world away from the totalitarianism that had existed under Stalin. The current situation, however, is precarious. Although there has not been a return to the terror of the Stalin era, efforts at liberalization in the Soviet Union and her satellites have been slow and are often stymied by the conservative leadership. Nowhere in the Communist world are the civil liberties of the people respected. One positive step has been the signing on August 1, 1975, of the Helsinki Agreement. *(See Reading No. 30.)* In this document the United States and Canada joined the nations of Europe (except Albania) in agreeing to respect "human rights and fundamental freedoms." There is no evidence however that the government of the Soviet Union and her satellites have attempted to implement this understanding. But the document has provided a basis of appeal for East European dissidents.

**The "Prague Spring."** Symbolic of the struggle for human rights in Communist Eastern Europe was the attempt made in Czechoslovakia in early 1968 to create "democratic socialism." Despite its prewar tradition of parliamentary democracy, from 1948 to 1968 Czechoslovakia suffered under one of the most repressive Communist governments in Eastern Europe. The dictator Antonin Novotny showed little inclination to liberalize his regime. For many years he resisted demands by intellectuals for civil liberties, intellectual freedom, and political democracy.

On January 5, 1968, Alexander Dubcek was elected as first secretary of the Czechoslovak Communist party. Dubcek's election was a victory for those forces which favored liberalization of the regime. In the months after Dubcek's election a wave of reform swept the country. Censorship of the press was relaxed, political prisoners were "rehabilitated," foreign travel was made easier, new student organizations appeared, and trade unions asserted greater independence. There were even demands for opposition political parties and the churches made an attempt to assert their rights.

Dubcek and the moderate Communists associated with him were uneasy with much that was taking place in the country. Dubcek had advocated "Socialism with a human face." But many workers and intellectuals saw his program as half-way democracy. In April 1968, the long-heralded

Action Program of the Czechoslovak Communist Party came as a disappointment to many progressives in the country. In June, a group of writers and intellectuals issued the famous *Two Thousand Words*. This manifesto was a direct challenge to the authority of the Communist Party. It boldly stated that as far as credit for the democratization policy "no thanks therefore, are due to the Communist Party." It criticized the Communist Party leadership as a group which had become the new aristocracy, taking the place of the old ruling class.

However, what was most characteristic of the "Prague Spring" was the surprisingly rational atmosphere which made possible a comparatively calm discussion between the party leadership and the people. In contrast to Hungary in 1956, there was no organized anti-Socialist or anti-Soviet movement in the country. The aim of the reform leadership was the creation of a Socialist society which would respect the human rights aspirations of the people. All understood that Czechoslovakia would have to remain as a satellite of the U.S.S.R.

**The Soviet Invasion of Czechoslovakia.** The leaders of the Soviet Union and the other satellite states looked with alarm at developments in Czechoslovakia. Supposedly, they feared that Czechoslovakia would become a pro-Western or neutralist state that would threaten their security. However, what disturbed the Soviet leaders was the example which Czechoslovak "democratic-socialism" would create for the peoples of the other satellite states and ultimately for the Soviet people themselves. If the Czech experiment had succeeded the agitation for reform in the Communist bloc would have been irresistible. The inevitable result of this liberalization would have been the end of the Communist party's monopoly of power which the men in the Kremlin could never accept.

On August 21, 1968, Soviet troops with contingents from Poland, Bulgaria, East Germany, and Hungary (Rumania did not participate) invaded Czechoslovakia without warning or provocation. The Czech armed forces did not block the invasion. In attempting to justify their attack, the Soviets announced their own version of natural law. They asserted that their action was motivated by the necessity to "protect Socialism" which is the highest imperative to which all other rights and laws are subordinated. This philosophy represented a total rejection of the concept of human rights that evolved in the Western and every other cultural tradition.

The Soviet troops were told that they were being sent to "liberate" Czechoslovakia. Some of these troops were embarrassed and ashamed when they saw the brave yet nonviolent resistance of the Czech people. In the absence of the Czech political leaders who were held in Moscow, the radio, television, and the press rallied the people. From cladestine transmitters and with mimeographed issues of newspapers, the people were told the truth about the invasion and were directed in their resistance measures.

On August 22, 1968, the Czechs were even able to organize a secret Communist Party Congress which 1192 out of 1543 delegates were able to attend. The Congress condemned the invasion, demanded the withdrawal of the troops, and the release of the country's leaders. It was a tribute to the resistance of the Czech people that the Soviets were unable to organize a quisling puppet regime. Eventually, Dubcek and his colleagues were released by the Russians who were forced to negotiate with men whom they had branded as counterrevolutionaries. The Soviets were unable to find any traitors who would come forward to negotiate with them. The unity of the Czech people and the heroism of their resistance was a testament to the will of a people who wanted to remain free.

**The Post-Invasion Repression.** Soon, however, the overwhelming military power of the Soviets proved impossible for the Czechs to resist. In the weeks and months that followed the invasion, most of the reforms were rescinded. On August 31, 1968, a ban on non-Communist political organizations was announced. In September, censorship was officially reimposed and the right of assembly was restricted. On October 16, 1968, a Soviet-Czechoslovak treaty was signed which provided that an unspecified number of Soviet troops would remain in Czechoslovakia for an unspecified period of time. About 80,000 Soviet troops are believed to be still in the country.

**Charter 77.** After the invasion, the regime carried on a campaign of "normalization" which involved continuing sanctions against a large part of the population. In early 1977, a number of Czech intellectuals drew up Charter 77 which protested the violations of the Helsinki Agreement which were taking place in their country. Many gifted and creative people were denied employment in their professions because they disagreed with official policy. Even a minor deviation from established ideology—political, philosophical, scientific, or artistic—brought reprisals. Many young people were denied access to higher education because of their parents' political past. Charter 77 also protested against the absence of freedom of religion. Religious instruction was being discouraged and the clergy feared the loss of the necessary government permission to exercise their office.

The persecution of those who signed Charter 77 proves that the allegations made in the document are true. The secret police arrested the three men who were designated to deliver the Charter to the government before they reached their destination. Another signer of the declarration, the 71-year-old distinguished philosopher Dr. Jan Patocka, died shortly after he was arrested by the political police. His crime was attempting to inform a foreign diplomat about the Charter 77 movement. In the fall of 1979, many other signers of the Charter were arrested by the police. Survivors of the "Prague Spring" and the Charter 77 movement are subject to constant surveillance and harassment. The Communist leadership is paranoid about the possible action of dissidents who represent the sentiments of the great mass of the population.

**Poland.** Russia's largest East European satellite, Poland, is a constant source of anxiety to the Kremlin.

Perhaps nowhere else in the world are the people so much out of sympathy with the system under which they are forced to live. Communism is seen by most Poles as an alien ideology which was imposed on them by Soviet military power after World War II. The people of Poland bitterly resent the government's denial of their economic, religious, and political rights. In 1970, the country was rocked by workers' strikes along the Baltic coast. These outbreaks led to the downfall of the government of Party Secretary Wladyslaw Gomulka.

There were further disturbances in June 1976. Workers set fire to the Communist Party headquarters in the city of Radom while other rioters tore up the tracks on Poland's main railroad line. The angry mobs were protesting a government announcement of a food price rise on many important commodities. The government ordered the arrest of the protest leaders who were threatened with trials for sedition. A committee for the defense of workers was organized. The human rights advocates on this committee were arrested and charged with fostering bourgeois ideological sabotage.

A principal factor in the Polish situation is the Roman Catholic Church which is actively supported by the overwhelming majority of the people. The election of a Polish Cardinal as Pope John Paul II in December 1978 emphasized the important role of the Catholic Church in Polish life. The Church is one of the chief protectors of human rights in contemporary Poland. It remains one of the few places where there is freedom of opinion and a limited amount of free speech. The clergy do not receive government stipends as in some other East European countries. Despite their economic problems, the Polish people give generous voluntary offerings to the Church. There is even a Roman Catholic University at Lublin which receives no government funds but is supported by the people.

Until recently, outside the sanctuary of the Church, few human rights have been recognized in Poland. Meetings of dissidents have been raided by the police. There is a secret police who use torture on political prisoners. The government carried on an economic policy including high prices for meat and other food items which was bitterly resented by the workers. It was not surprising that in August 1980 workers in Gdansk and other Polish cities went on strike. They demanded important concessions in both the realm of economic and human rights. *(See Reading No. 31.)* On August 31, 1980, an agreement was reached in which the government made important concessions. Relatively free labor unions were recognized as well as the right to strike. The government also promised to limit censorship and to free many political prisoners. The position of the Church in Poland was further strengthened. But in December 1981, the Polish government moved to halt the reform movement, which was a signal to all East European dissidents.

## LATIN AMERICA

As in Africa and Asia, most of the population of Latin America live in extreme poverty. This situation is perpetuated by high rates of illiteracy, disease, and rigid class barriers. Many countries are ruled by military oligarchies which represent the interests of a small group of wealthy landowners and industrialists. These people greatly fear left-wing revolutionaries. The existence of Marxist terrorists is used as the rationale to justify severe repression. Rule by decree extends emergency powers indefinitely. In many countries there are massive arrests not only of leftist terrorists but also of journalists, intellectuals, and students who favor moderate reform. Many countries have secret police forces which are used to suppress suspected leftist terrorists. There is often also a considerable amount of right-wing terrorism in many Latin American countries aimed at leftists, liberals, and even moderates who wish to compromise with the reformers. In some countries, there is a pattern of torture, kidnapping, and murder by government and right-wing terrorists against the left which leads to counterreprisals by Marxist terrorists in an unending cycle. In such an atmosphere the protection of basic human rights becomes impossible.

For several decades, the existence of a Communist government in Cuba has served as an inspiration for the leftist opposition in many countries. Unfortunately, the extreme left in Latin America has not shown any more respect for human rights than the governments they seek to overthrow. Such ideas as open elections, an opposition press, academic freedom, and religious toleration are as alien to the extreme left in Latin America as in other parts of the world. The flight of almost one million people from Cuba, including 120,000 in the summer of 1980, gives some indication of the Marxist attitude in Latin America toward human rights.

**Guatemala.** Recently the small nations of Central America have become battlegrounds of the extreme right and left. In July 1979, the repressive right-wing dictatorship of Anastasio Samoza in Nicaragua was overthrown. The Marxist regime which came to power undertook a massive campaign of reform which relied heavily on aid from Castro's Cuba. In some areas such as education there has been praiseworthy progress. But there are signs that basic civil and political rights are being violated.

The success of the guerillas in Nicaragua has given considerable encouragement to rebels in other Central American countries. This is especially true of Guatemala, the largest country in the region. Terrorism is not new in Guatemala. Atrocities of extreme left and right have been common for several decades. There has been a great intensification of such activity on both sides.

The root cause of the problem is enormous social inequality which is suffered by the vast majority of the population while a privileged minority live in great luxury. On a recent holiday in Guatemala the author went on a guided tour of the capital. The guide was a young student. When we came to an imposing government building, he said: "Here is the Palace of Justice. As you can see there is much palace but very little justice." There is a great deal of evidence to support this statement particularly for the Indians who comprise 55 percent of the population. Indeed, a recent United Nations report indicates that Guatemala's Indians have a standard of living comparable to the poorest in Bangladesh or Somalia. Overpopulation has created a situation where the primitive Indian methods of cultivation can no longer support the increasing size of families. More and more Indians are forced to work on the white man's plantations where they are brutally cheated and mistreated. In Guatemala the stoic Indian is rebelling in a society where he is treated as less than human.

Many Indians are supporting the extreme leftist guerrillas. This has set off tremors of fear among the privileged whites who have their own terrorist groups which are universally believed to be supported by the government. Terrorism has reached epidemic proportions. The fields of politics, journalism, and even the priesthood have become high-risk occupations. In its attacks on the leftist rebels the government troops give no quarter. Trials of terrorists are rare since summary executions are common. It is said that there are no political prisoners in Guatemala since all are dead.

The United States faces a difficult problem in deciding whether to support repressive right-wing governments such as the regime in Guatemala. Failure to support such a government could result in the victory for the Marxists who would be equally repressive as well as hostile to American interests. However, aid to right-wing dictatorships costs the United States considerable support in the Third World. The attitude adopted by the Reagan administration toward Guatemala will help set the pattern for American policy toward right-wing governments throughout the world.

**Chile.** Unlike most other Latin American countries, Chile has a long tradition of democratic government. Academic freedom, a thriving press, and vigorously contested free elections have characterized its history. In 1970, the Marxist Salvador Allende was elected President. He

accelerated the process of land reform and government
nationalization which had begun with his Christian Democratic predecessors. The conservative forces in Chile greatly feared Allende. With American support, a military coup
in 1973 toppled the Allende government. It is difficult
to say if Allende had remained in office whether he would
have respected the civil and political rights of the Chilean
people. It is possible he would have turned in the direction of Castro's Cuba, since he was on very friendly terms
with that government. Nonetheless Allende did initiate
economic and social reforms that benefited the impover-
sihed masses in the country.

Since the anti-Allende coup in 1973, Chile has been
under the rule of a military regime headed by General
Augusto Pinochet. Immediately after the coup, the supporters of Allende were rounded up and brutally punished. In the years since then, there have been frequent
reports of repressive measures taken by the Pinochet
regime. Chile's secret police, the DINA, is one of the most
feared security forces in Latin America. There seems little
hope for any liberalization in the near future. In September 1980, in a national plebiscite voters approved a new
constitution and eight-and-a-half more years of military
rule by General Pinochet.

**The United Nations and Human Rights.** The United
Nations has an obvious role to play in the protection of
human rights. Despite ideological and regional divisions
of its membership, the world organization can be used as
a forum for the discussion of human rights issues. On
December 16, 1966, the General Assembly approved the
Covenant of Economic, Social, and Cultural Rights *(see
Reading No. 32)* and the Covenant on Civil and Political
Rights *(see Reading No. 33)*. Both, however, required
ratification by thirty-five member states. This occurred
for the Covenant on Economic, Social, and Cultural
Rights on January 3, 1976, and for the Covenant on Civil
and Political Rights on March 23, 1976. In October 1977,
the United States signed both documents.

A hopeful sign with regard to these Covenants is that both contain provisions for measures of implementation. Each member state who signs the Covenant agress to submit reports to the United Nations Commission on Human Rights and to the pertinent special agencies. The comments of these bodies will be considered by the U.N. Economic and Social Council which will then make its own recommendations for submission to the General Assembly. Under the Covenant on Civil and Political Rights, there is a provision for a new Human Rights Committee of eighteen members serving in a personal capacity which will study the reports submitted to the member states. The Human Rights Committee will draw up an annual report of its activities which will ultimately be submitted to the General Assembly. It is hoped that these U.N. committees will eventually have an impact on the worldwide problem of human rights violations.

# 10

# PROTESTS MOVEMENTS IN THE UNITED STATES

**The Human Rights Revolution.** Beginning in the 1950s, there has been a movement to end discrimination against black people in the United States. The success of this civil rights struggle has encouraged other groups to make an effort to win all the rights to which they are entitled as American citizens and as members of the human race. Minorities, such as the Hispanics and Indians, are working for a recognition of their civil, political, social, and economic rights. Many women's groups have sprung up to continue the feminist struggle which was begun in the nineteenth century. The rights of children, the elderly, and the handicapped have also become public issues. If all these groups are successful, the ultimate result will be a society in which every American will have the opportunity to live a full productive life. Although it is not possible to describe each of these movements in detail, we can outline the struggle which has been waged by some of the human rights groups in our country.

**The Civil Rights Movement.** Probably the most important protest movement in this country in modern times has been the demand by black people for their civil, political, economic, and social rights as American citizens. As late as 1945, in one-third of the states, people with dark skins were excluded from most decent schools, restaurants, and public parks. They were confined to the rear of buses and to separate railroad cars. Black people could not vote in most elections in the South and even in the North were largely limited to menial employment. The armed forces of the United States were segregated. In Washington, D.C., with its numerous foreign embassies, a black person could not sit at a drugstore lunch counter or visit a movie house in the downtown area.

There were many factors in the post World War II era which were creating the conditions for change in American race relations. The industrialization and urbanization of the South created a cosmopolitan atmosphere in which segregation seemd out of place. There was also the impact of television and other mass media which tended to weaken regional differences thoughout the country. Gradually, there was a growth in legal and political protection for the Negro.

In 1948, there were the first signs that a major change was about to take place in American life. In two executive orders President Harry Truman ended segregation and discrimination in the armed forces and in all agencies and departments of the federal government. The overwhelming turnout of blacks in the Northern states to support Truman in the hotly contested election of 1948 showed that blacks could use the franchise to reward or punish politicians based on their civil rights records. Between 1948 and 1954, slow but steady progress was made in the area of human rights for black Americans. In 1950, segregation of blacks in dining cars on interstate railroads was banned as an undue burden on interstate commerce. In 1953, the United States Supreme Court, basing its decision on an 1872 statute, ordered all restaurants in the nation's capital to serve patrons regardless of race, creed, or color.

**The Brown Decision.** In the early 1950s, there were steady gains by blacks to end segregation in the Southern educational system. Legal victories were won in Tennessee, Missouri, Kentucky, Louisiana, and North Carolina. By far the most important of these cases was the one involving Texas. In its ruling in *Sweatt vs. Texas,* the Court virtually killed the separate but equal doctrine. All that now remained was its internment and this in due course was accomplished in *Brown vs. Board of Education* on May 17, 1954.

The *Brown* case marked the end of an era. In its decision in the case, the United States Supreme Court invalidated statutes in seventeen states that compelled school

segregation by law and those in four other states and the
District of Columbia that permitted it. Blacks were at
first overjoyed by this decision which many believed
would immediately end segregation. However, white
Southerners organized themselves for firm resistance.
White Citizens Councils sprang up all over the South.
These and other groups were resolved that no desegregation should take place in their communities. On December
29, 1955, Senator James A. Eastland of Mississippi
formed the Federation for Constitutional Government. In
keeping with its determination to mount a massive resistance against the *Brown* decision, the Federation promulgated a document commonly known as the *Southern
Manifesto* which it presented to the United States Congress on March 12, 1956. The Manifesto commended the
"motives of those States which have declared the intention to resist forced integration by any lawful means."

Other methods used to resist desegregation included
economic pressure on blacks and white moderates who
advocated compliance with the Supreme Court decision.
State legislatures revived the doctrine of interposition
which supposedly gave states the right to reject or nullify
federal laws which they believed violated the Constitution. Some Southern officials threatened the mass closure
of public schools rather than compliance with the *Brown*
decision. White private "academies" were founded in
some areas to take the place of the public schools. There
was considerable and protracted litigation in many areas
to stall and delay the implementation of desegregation.
Very often violence and intimidation was used to bar
blacks from actually attending white schools.

Indeed, in almost every state in the South there were
violent incidents when blacks attempted to register at
all-white schools. In September 1957, nine black students
attempted to integrate Central High School in Little
Rock, Arkansas. Governor Orval Faubus ordered the
Arkansas National Guard to turn back the black students.
The National Guard did nothing to protect the black
students or to quell the mob violence. Such outbreaks of

civil disorder on the part of segregationists turned Northern opinion in favor of the Supreme Court decision. Southern extremism did more than arouse Northern opinion; it aroused the federal government. President Eisenhower had planned to do nothing to support the rights of blacks until Governor Faubus and the mob at Little Rock forced his administration to take action. The President sent 1,000 federal troops to Little Rock to escort the black students to school. Eisenhower acted because he believed that no President could allow open defiance of federal law by state officials. After the Little Rock incident, in the last three years of the Eisenhower admistration, there was a subtle shift on the part of the federal government in favor of desegration, but major progress did not come until the 1960s.

**Martin Luther King, Jr.**   The son and grandson of Baptist preachers, Martin Luther King was destined for the ministry from an early age. In January 1954, he became pastor of the Dexter Avenue Baptist Church in Montogmery, Alabama. In December 1955, a black woman, Mrs. Rosa Parks, refused to give up her seat to a white man on a segregated bus in Montgomery. Mrs. Parks was arrested and ordered to trial on charges of violating segregation laws. Under the leadership of Dr. Martin Luther King, Jr., the blacks of Montgomery organized a boycott of the segregated bus system. Although still in his twenties, Dr. King showed unusually mature judgment, definite leadership qualities, and an unparalleled gift for public speaking. He wisely insisted that black people must end segregation through nonviolent protest. Like Mohandas Gandhi who ended British rule in India through nonviolent protest, Dr. King believed that nonviolence could be a powerful weapon to mobilize public sympathy for the black cause. The protest movement took on a dynamism of a religious crusade bringing to bear the full weight of the Christian church which was the strongest emotional force in the black community. The stubborn sacrifice and determination of the blacks earned them the grudging respect of even some of their white antagonists.

For almost a year, the blacks of Montgomery walked to work or participated in car pools rather than ride on segregated buses. This protest gained national attention and soon there were bus boycotts in many other Southern cities. Black people showed that they could win their rights in a calm, deliberate, and dignified manner which belied the slander of their racist detractors. Finally, on November 13, 1956, the Supreme Court ruled that segregation violated the Constitution. A few weeks later all over the South blacks and whites could ride buses on an equal basis.

A major consequence of the Montgomery experience was to capitulate Martin Luther King, Jr. into the role of leader of the struggle against segregation. In February 1957, black preachers from ten states of the Deep South assembled in New Orleans and established a new organization to be known as the Southern Christian Leadership Conference (SCLC). Martin Luther King, Jr. was elected president and his nonviolence formula was adopted as a basic blueprint for the new group.

**Student Activists.** The next major phase of the civil rights movement was initiated by black students from various Southern colleges who admired and implemented the ideas and tactics of Martin Luther King, Jr. On February 1, 1960, Ezell Blair and Joseph McNeill attempted a "sit-in" at a lunch counter in Greensboro, North Carolina. Thus began a movement which soon spread to Virginia, Tennessee, South Carolina, and Georgia. The decision to stage a "sit-in" was invariably made by a handful of student activists who were able to pull in a large number of colleagues after the initial thrust. Despite its spontaneity, however, the movement did observe one common and binding principle—strict adherence to the practice of nonviolence.

Atlanta, Georgia, was the scene of one of the largest sit-in campaigns. In anticipation of a possible sit-in demonstration, the Georgia legislature had enacted an antitrespass law which made it illegal for people not to leave a premise when ordered to do so. This did not discourage the students of Atlanta's colleges who planned to desegregate the city. The students drew up "An Appeal to Human Rights" and began sit-ins in cafeterias, lunch counters of municipal and state buildings, and restaurants in railroad and bus terminals. Seventy-six students were arrested for violation of the month-old antitrespass law. There were sympathy demonstrations in the North and a boycott of national chains which ran segregated outlets in the South. Among the groups which emerged to national prominence during the sit-in campaign was the Student Non-Violent Coordinating Committee. SNCC was a student-run organization which advocated that the young people themselves should coordinate and direct their own demonstrations.

The next major phase of the civil rights struggle was an effort to desegregate interstate travel. On March 13, 1961, the Congress of Racial Equality (CORE) announced that it would conduct "Freedom Rides" throughout the South to challenge segregation in bus depots and terminals. SNCC also joined in this effort to use peaceful protest to implement a ruling by the Interstate Commerce Commission that interstate travel be desegregated. Some of the "Freedom Riders" were attacked by militant segregationists. In May 1961, it became necessary for Attorney-General Robert Kennedy to order U.S. marshals to protect the black and white young people who sought to exercise their constitutional rights.

**Birmingham 1963.** In early 1963, the black leadership of Birmingham, Alabama, asked Dr. Martin Luther King, Jr. for his assistance in the campaign to end segregation in their community. The streets, water supply, and sewer systems were about the only public facilities shared by both black and white in this thoroughly segregated city. Matters were compounded by the recent election of George Wallace as Governor of Alabama on an ultra-segregationist platform. Dr. King described Birmingham as "a community in which human rights had been trampled for so long that fear and oppression were as thick in its atmosphere as the smog from its factories." The Reverend Fred Lee Shuttleworth of the Alabama Christian Movement for Human Rights outlined the demands of the black community which were exceedingly modest. This program included the removal of racial restrictions in downtown snack bars, rest rooms, and stores; the adoption of nonracial hiring practices for such posts as salesgirl and secretary; and the formation of a biracial committee to carry on continuing negotiations for further desegregation.

Dr. King and his associates were opposed by the Birmingham police chief, "Bull" Connor, one of the most strident racists in the South. In the presence of hordes of newsmen and camera crews, Connor used snapping, snarling police dogs and fire hoses on the peacefully demonstrating black men, women, and children. Pictures of this brutality were shown throughout the world. The nation was shocked. President Kennedy took an active interest in the situation and arranged for the release of Dr. King from a Birmingham jail. On May 26, the United States Supreme Court declared Alabama's law on segregation to be unconstitutional.

Governor Wallace, however, was determined to keep his election promise to "stand in the schoolhouse door" to prevent the integration of Alabama's schools. When the federal district court ordered the University of Alabama to admit two black students, Wallace vowed his intention of defying the federal government. On June 11, when the two black students came to the University of Alabama to register, Governor Wallace stood in the doorway and gave them a "stop" signal with his outstretched hand. President Kennedy immediately reacted by sending in federalized National Guardsmen to assure the registration of the black students. That evening Kennedy spoke to the nation in one of the most significant speeches in the history of the American presidency. *(See Reading No. 34.)* He was attempting to use the moral influence of his office to support the movement for black equality.

**The March on Washington.**    President Kennedy, however, was uneasy about the March on Washington which was planned in the summer of 1963. It was feared that a disorderly demonstration by blacks in the capital could do a great deal of havoc to the black cause. At a White House meeting on June 23, Kennedy tried to dissuade black leaders from holding the massive demonstration. But with the financial assistance of sixty-five corporations and foundations, the black leaders decided to proceed with the March on Wasshington. With its galaxy of dignitaries and celebrities on the raised platform and some 200,000 people assembled before them at the Lincoln Memorial, the March on Washington was easily one of the most significant demonstrations ever to be held in the nation's Capital. The fears about disorder and violence were not realized. The crowd was good natured but the underlying tone was one of dead seriousness. The march leaders met with President Kennedy who issued a statement praising the marchers for the "deep fervor and quiet dignity" that had characterized the demonstration. The high point of the March on Washington was the address by Dr. King. His "I Have a Dream" speech has come down as an eloquent statement on human rights.

**Civil Rights Legislation.**    From th earliest days of the civil rights movement, it was apparent that federal legislation would be necessary to force many of the Southern states and municipalities to grant equal rights to their black citizens. The Civil Rights Act of 1957 was the first piece of legislation on civil rights to pass the Congress since Reconstruction. It allowed the Justice Department to bring suits on behalf of blacks who had been denied the right to vote. It also set up a Civil Rights Commission and a Civil Rights Division in the Justice Department. On June 19, 1963, President Kennedy sent a comprehensive civil rights bill to Congress. On November 22, 1963, President Kennedy was assassinated and was succeeded by Lyndon B. Johnson of Texas. While Senate majority leader, Johnson had played a key role in the passage of the Civil Rights Bills of 1957. As President, he vigorously attempted to push new civil rights legislation through Congress. On July 2, 1964, he was able to sign into law the bill originally proposed by President Kennedy. The Civil Rights Act of 1964 banned discrimination in hotels and places of entertainment. The Attorney General was authorized to initiate suits on behalf of individuals in school integration cases. There were also provision to insure fair employment and voter registration.

Even more revolutionary was the Federal Voting Rights Act of 1965 which provided for direct federal intervention to enable blacks to register and vote. There was no longer any need to resort to courts and to engage in protracted litigation. The act also suspended literacy tests and other discriminatory requirements in the six Southern States of Alabama, Georgia, Louisiana, South Carolina, Mississippi, and Virginia. Federal examiners were sent into these states where they uncovered and discontinued many of the practices used since Reconstruction to prevent blacks from voting.

**Black Militancy.** Not all blacks accepted the philosophy of nonviolence. Many felt that a true revolution was necessary in order to gain equality in America. In 1966, Stokley Carmichael gained prominence with his use of the term Black Power. His election as chairman of SNCC was symbolic of the turn away from nonviolence on the part of many young blacks. During this period there were major riots in many American cities including Los Angeles, Chicago, Newark, and Detroit. Although Dr. King refused to abandon nonviolence, he began to take a much more militant position. He spoke of the need for "massive changes" and described the white power structure as "evil and corrupt." He shifted his focus to economic issues. In early 1968, he planned a "Poor Peoples Campaign" to converge on Washington, D.C., on April 22, 1968. The objective was the enactment of an "Economic Bill of Rights for the Disadvantaged" which he hoped Congress would pass in order to lift blacks and other minorities out of the cycle of poverty.

Before launching the "Poor Peoples Campaign" Dr. King visited Memphis, Tennessee, in order to give his assistance to a strike of black public works and sanitation employees. On April 4, 1968, Dr. King was shot and killed by James Earl Ray. This assassination touched off riots in 125 American cities and towns. With the death of Martin Luther King, Jr. the door was flung open to the apostles of violence. For several years America feared open rebellion by black nationalists, separatists, and terrorists. Fortunately, no such nationwide rebellion took place but the civil rights movement was seriously hampered.

**Recent Developments.** During the 1970s and early 1980s, the focus of the struggle for black equality switched to such issues as school busing, affirmative action, and quotas. In many parts of the country where segregation was not mandated by law, *de facto* segregation in schooling existed because of housing patterns. Many blacks wished to impose a system of busing children in order to create a "racial balance" in inner city school systems. This effort was opposed by most whites and a considerable minority of black parents. Also controversial has been the effort to set quotas mandating the hiring or admittance into professional schools of a certain percentage of black applicants. Giving preference to black applicants, known as affirmative action, has also encountered opposition. In the *Bakke* case of 1978 the Supreme Court upheld the constitutionality of affirmative action but further litigation on the subject is expected.

Though considerable problem areas exist, progress made in race relations over the past three decades should not be overlooked. Blacks enjoy opportunities and privileges that were unthinkable in previous generations. Even in the Deep South, all public education has been desegregated. Blacks make up a sizable portion of the electorate in most Southern states and have influenced many electtions. Such cities as Los Angeles, Atlanta, Detroit, and Newark have elected black mayors. There has been a virtual explosion in the number of blacks who have been graduated from colleges all over the country. The percentage of blacks in almost every kind of white-collar employment has steadily increased despite the recent bad times economically. There is every reason to expect further progress in the future.

**Native Americans.**   American Indians are another minority who in recent years have waged a struggle to attain their legitimate rights. The main focus of their efforts has been legal action to secure their rights and benefits spelled out in treaties and agreements made by Indian tribes with the United States government. These documents have been negotiated over a period of hundreds of years. Some of these covenants go back as far as the American Revolution. This battle has been carried on tribe by tribe and by various Pan-Indian organizations such as the American Indian Movement (AIM) and the National Congress of American Indians (NCAI).

Most surviving Indian tribes have made some treaty or legal agreement with the United States government. Many native Americans are distrubed that these legally binding documents have been flagrantly violated by business interests and all levels of government. These violations include default of monetary compensation and failure to provide stipulated services such as health care and schools. However, the major problem has been the unwarranted seizure of Indian lands. This is particularly disturbing to native Americans because to all tribes the land is sacred. Indians revere the land and this feeling for the land is a characteristic that is basic to all tribes in every part of the country. Among the important cases which Indians have fought have been the disputes over the Blue Lake region in New Mexico, the land claims by native Americans in Alaska, and the struggle of the Sioux to regain the Black Hills region of South Dakota. Significant legal victories have been won in many of these cases.

In order to dramatize their struggle, American Indians sometimes used militant tactics. In November 1969, a group of Indians, mostly university students in the San

Francisco Bay Area, took over the island of Alcatraz and proclaimed their intention of turning it into a cultural-education center. *(See Reading No. 35.)* In 1973, another group of native Americans including members of AIM occupied Wounded Knee, South Dakota, where they were confronted by the FBI, United States marshals and military personnel. Wounded Knee is particularly symbolic to native Americans since it was on this site that men, women, and children of the Sioux nation were massacred by the United States cavalry on December 29, 1890. Fortunately, the 1973 incident ended with far less bloodshed.

A current problem for native Americans is the desire of many energy companies to mine coal on Indian lands. The Hopi, Crow, Blackfoot, Navajo and Cheyenne, and various other tribes are determined to resist the destruction of their land and what may be the end of their traditional way of life. Some Indian activists have referred to this as "America's Final Act of Genocide." The remaining Indian tribes in this country represent only a small fraction of the tribes that existed before the arrival of the white man. It is hoped that they will retain the right to live on their own land in the traditional manner if they so desire.

**The Women's Movement.** In the 1970s there was a worldwide interest in women's rights and the place of women in society. Such issues as abortion, divorce laws, and sex discrimination in employment received prominent attention in the news media. It is, of course, impossible to pinpoint the beginning of the modern phase of the feminist movement but publication of Betty Friedan's *The Feminine Mystique* in 1963 had a profound effect on the thinking of many women. Friedan asserted that women were dissatisfied with their role as housewife-mother which did not offer them total fulfillment as human beings. She suggested that the solution for overcoming this problem was for women to find employment outside the home.

In 1966, women all over the country organized the National Organization of Women (NOW) with Betty

Friedan as president. The aim of the organization was "true equality for all women in American . . . as part of the world-wide revolution of human rights." NOW works locally and nationally on court cases and legislative, lobbying on matters of reproduction and child care and on opening up opportunities for women in the job market. Its ultimate aim is that 51 percent of leadership positions in government, industry, and the professions should be held by women since they make up 51 percent of the population.

In 1971, the National Women's Political Caucus (NWPC) was formed in Washington, D.C. The principal goal of this organization is to support women who are running for public office on the local and national level. NWPC also has a wide-ranging program *(see Reading No. 36)* aimed at improving the status of women in every area of life. Both NWPC and NOW have been strong supporters of the Equal Rights Amendment to the Constitution. The proposed Twenty-Seventh Amendment reads, "Equality of rights under the law shall not be denied or abridged by the United States or by any state on account of sex." In 1972, the ERA was passed by both houses of Congress. It was sent to the states for ratification. By 1979, however, it has not been ratified by a sufficient number of states to become law. The seven-year time limit for ratification has been extended in the hope that ratification by three-fourths of the states can be achieved.

Some of the groups in the feminist movement take a much more radical approach to the problem of women's place in contemporary society. These groups oppose the monogamous family and see women as an oppressed class. Men are seen as the enemy and responsible for most of the problems plaguing contemporary civilization. However, the main thrust of the women's movement remains intent on improving the relationship between men and women by creating a truly equal partnership between the sexes.

**The Handicapped.** Perhaps the people in our society who have been most consistently denied the right to lead full productive lives are the handicapped. Fortunately, they are one of the groups which have been most affected by the human rights revolution and are now vocally demanding their rightful place in society. Disabled people can be found in all ethnic and economic groups. It is estimated that about 22 million Americans have "physical impariments which restrict their normal daily activity." Traditionally, they have had low visibility since the lack of opportunities for them have often made handicapped people prisoners in their own homes. Because of laws against seeing eye dogs and physical barriers such as stairs and narrow doorways which bar people in wheel chairs, disabled people have not been able to attend school or obtain productive employment.

For many years the courts upheld discrimination against the handicapped. They were legally barred from public schools as students and often as teachers. A blind person who was involved in an accident was held to be negligent for leaving his home by himself. The aim of the public policy was one of "benevolent paternalism" which would protect handicapped people and allow them to live in seclusion with as little pain or discomfort as possible. The present movement to achieve equal rights for handicapped persons reflects not only a change in national public policy toward handicapped persons, but also a change in the attitudes of handicapped persons themselves from defensiveness and inferiority to self-acceptance and assertiveness.

In large measure through their own lobbying efforts, handicapped people have won significant victories by securing passage of civil rights legislation for disabled people. A major step was passage of the Architectural Barriers Act of 1968 which marked the dawn of a new era in federal policy toward handicapped persons. This law made it obligatory for government buildings and buildings financed by the United States government grants or loans to be made accessible to the handicapped. Another important piece of legislation was the Rehabilitation Act of 1973 which mandated that handicapped people should not be discriminated against in any program receiving federal financial assistance. This act also provided for "affirmative action" in the employment and advancement of qualified handicapped individuals by many federal contractors.

Many of the federal bills which were originally passed to protect racial minorities have been extended to include coverage of the handicapped. In Illinois, Indiana, New York, and Washington, state civil rights legislation has been amended to cover disabled people. A model civil rights act for handicapped people was passed in Michigan in 1976. Despite these successes, further advances are required if handicapped people are to function as free and equal members of our society. The cost of making more buildings and public transporation accessible to the handicapped is very great. More lobbying is necessary to win additional victories in a period of financial austerity.

**Children's Rights.**   In the nineteenth and early twentieth century, an effort was made to protect children through child labor and mandatory school attendance legislation. This effort has generally proven to be successful. However, the contemporary children's rights movement seeks to rectify injustices of a different type.

Few will argue against the removal of children from hard labor in dirty, unsafe factories and the subsitution of compulsory education to enable a better and easier method of support in adulthood. Yet, advocates point out that this situation has created new problems. Compulsory education and denial of the right to work at an early age has made the child dependent on the parent or its insititutional subsitute for a far longer period of time, with little say in how that time will be spent. If parent and child are in agreement on the question of lifestyle there is little problem. But for the abused, neglected, or differing child these added years can be torture. A parent's rights over a child are almost absolute. He can force a child to practice a religion he does not believe in, control his friends, the way he dresses, his schooling, where he will live and with whom (not necessarily the parent), medical care, the right to drive, what the child will receive in the mail, employment and even sex.

The children's rights movment does not deny the parent's responsibilities and the special circumstances that children are in. It aims to guarantee for children certain basic rights that belong to all humans and cannot and should not be governed by a parent. These include control of one's own body, the right to adequate medical care both before and after birth, access to medical care that a parent may oppose, i.e., information and treatment of venereal disease, control of pregnancy either by abortion or maintaining a pregnancy that a parent may wish to terminate, consenting participation in sexual activity, refusal of behavior-altering drugs in school that parents may encourage.

The children's rights movement has also focused attention on the legal rights of children. The cornerstone of this system is the specialized courts and detention systems used only for juveniles. This system was supposedly devised to segregate and protect the miscreant child from the revolving doors of adult courts and prisons. Children were viewed as not responsible for their actions, no matter how criminal, but capable of reformation by maturity. Therefore, it was considered best for the child to have his criminal actions hidden from the public in special courts and sealed records that would not haunt his adult and presumably nondeviant years. This system has successfully kept the names of juvenile offenders from the headlines of newspapers but it has also kept th abridgment of their rights from public view. Juveniles are frequently convicted and incarcerated after juvenile hearings that have neither a jury nor defending counsel present for the child. In many states the "crimes" presented are "status offenses," that is, actions that are not considered to be crimes when committed by adults. Under these proceedings a child who is deemed incorrigible, unruly, or runaway by parents or officials can be commited to reform school or prison for such time as the court may see fit. Running away from abusive or otherwise unfit parents is not a valid defense in these proceedings.

A major victory for the children's rights movement was the *Gault* decision. In this important case, the Supreme Court ruled that a young suspect tried in juvenile court is entitled to have a lawyer, to cross-examine witnesses and to enjoy other safeguards guaranteed to adult defendants by the Constitution. By this decision the Court recognized for the first time that a child was a human being. *Gault* and other decisions are being used by the Juvenile Rights Project of the American Civil Liberties Union (ACLU) to end the system whereby children are treated as second-class citizens in juvenile courts.

An area of increasing concern to all civil libertarians is the question of access to records kept by various social agencies, government agencies, and private institutions. The adult rights to confidentiality and limited or no access and information sharing has been upheld in the courts. Yet most of the files kept on children are designed to be shared but without the subject's knowledge, review, or correction. Reports on behavior, personality, problems, as well as grades, are routinely kept by most schools and follow a child through the system. Such information is also routinely shared with juvenile courts and agencies charged with the care of children. Reports of court-appointed psychiatrists and probation officers are not confidential and may follow a child for life. Parents may also release damaging information without the consent of the child.

Many see the solution to these problems in economic terms. The extended adolescence existing in the industiral world creates an economic dependence on parents that usually lasts until the completion of at least high school but often through college. Our present laws support this and give parents the power to prevent a dependent from working. This prevents a child from taking responsibility for his own life however necessary it may be. A non-criminal but runaway child who is gainfully employed may still be incarcerated for the crime of leaving an intolerable home situation. Several states have passed laws giving limited emancipation to working teens under court supervision. This enables the abused, neglected, or sexually molested child to legally leave home if he or she can be self-supporting. But most employment available to these youths involves minimum wage and/or part-time jobs forcing a choice between school and work. It is the aim of the children's rights movement to make emancipation with the same resources available to unemployed adults available to all adolescents and change the work laws to have jobs limited by ability, not age.

**Homosexual Liberation.** Perhaps the most controversial human rights movement to gain prominence in recent years has been the effort by homosexuals to gain respect and consideration from their fellow Americans. For many years conservative nonconfrontational groups such as the Mattachine Society had been the only organizations representing the interests of homosexuals. But in the late 1960s many homosexuals who were active in the antiwar and other protest movements took an increasingly militant stance. This trend was greatly accentuated by the riot which took place on June 27, 1969, after police raided the Stonewall Inn in New York's Greenwich Village. This disturbance led to the formation of new organizations which demanded not only an end to police harassment but the implementation of a complete human rights program. Among the areas of concern to homosexuals are descrimination in employment, military service, housing, and child custody cases. The Gay Liberation Front and other militant organizations have won important legislative victories in many states and minicipalities where discrimination against homosexuals has been banned.

The opposition to the homosexual liberation movement has been exceedingly vocal, especially from some elements of the religious community. Many Americans fear that a permissive attitude toward homosexualty represents a threat to their family life, and is specifically prohibited by the Bible.

**Retrospect and Prospect.**  Man's struggle to attain individual rights has not been a story of uninterrupted advance. Throughout history there have been periods of stagnation, defeat, and retrogression. At times in certain societies the forces of tyranny seem to have achieved an absolute victory over the human spirit. But man's desire to assert his humanity has proven impossible for any despotism to suppress permantenly. In ancient times prophets and philosophers dreamed of a world where both men and nations would be free from the bondage of servitude. The struggle of the Hebrews against Egyptian, Babylonian, and Roman tyranny is symbolic of ancient man's instinctual impulse to assert his right to be free. The Greek inquiry into man's place in the world was in large measure an effort to define the rights of the individual within the framework of an orderly society. Siddhartha Gautama (Buddha) and Confucius were also deeply concerned about the preservation of individual rights and dignity. However, one of the tragedies of history is that each of the great religions have occasionally been perverted so that its teachings have been used to justify the suppression of human rights. In the European Middle Ages the Church suppressed freedom of conscience in the name of Christian unity and orthodoxy. All of the great religions have been used to justify wars and even outrageous atrocities.

As with religion, those who have claimed to favor political democracy have sometimes worked against human rights. The seventeenth- and eighteenth-century struggle for political and civil rights was not without its setbacks. During the French Revolution many innocent people were murdered by emotional mobs who justified their atrocities in the name of the "Rights of Man." Most of the leaders of the American Revolution saw no contradiction in fighting for their rights as Englishmen while denying the human rights of their black slaves.

In the neneteenth century the question of black slavery was an important issue in Western civilization. Although the institution of slavery was eventually terminated in Europe and America, the legacy of that problem still remains. The nineteenth-century reformers left the issue of the status of the freed blacks unresolved. Another key issue of the nineteenth century was the horrendous working conditions during the Industrial Revolution. The question of the standard of living of the proletariat has been resolved largely by the creation of an industrial society. But the dehumanization of the machine age has been intensified by the technological developments in the twentieth century.

Many scientific inventions such as mass communications, more rapid transportation, and improved methods of surveillance have made possible the totalitarian regimes of our century. In the totalitarian countries, technology is often the oppressor rather than the servant of man. In Stalinist Russia, millions of human beings worked and died as slave laborers on huge industrial projects where human life was expendable as long as the canal or hydroelectric plant was completed. Hitler used Europe's efficient railroad system and modern mass production techniques to exterminate millions of people.

In our own times, the irrational use of technology is a major threat to human rights. The biological revolution, with its dramatic breakthrough in genetics, may soon create a "Brave New World" in which the average man and woman will lose control of the reproduction process. There is also danger that the parameters of human life will become blurred, necessitating a perilous redefinition of human rights. Another danger is computer technology, which may place in the hands of government an unparalleled temptation to control the lives of the average citizen which could jeopardize the all-important right to individuality.

A very serious threat to human rights in our contemporary world is the present adverse economic situation, which has had the effect of lowering the standard of living of the poorest classes of society. Unless current financial trends are reversed, the economic and social rights which have been gained over the last century could be severely eroded. In our country, blacks and other minorities fear that they will be sacrificed in the austerity budgets of the 1980s. There is also fear that in the current climate the Voting Rights Act and other civil rights legislation which were won at such high cost will be repealed or diluted.

On the international scene, overreaction to the threat of terrorism may result in measures that will curtail individual rights in the effort to attain adequate security. The rights of free travel, privacy, free speech, and freedom of association are in danger of being sacrificed in the struggle against an admittedly genuine danger. Although international terrorism may necessitate prudent precautions, a substantial restriction of basic rights must be avoided, since the weakening of democratic institutions is the main goal of the terrorists.

Achieving an equitable standard of human rights for all individuals in any society has been and always will be an extremely difficult undertaking. But the effort is worth making. It is hoped that interest in human rights will not disappear. There are national and international human rights organizations in many countries. The existence of these organizations is a ray of hope in a world where the contraction rather than the expansion of individual rights is a frightening possibility.

# Part II

READINGS

# THE DECLARATION OF THE RIGHTS OF MAN AND THE CITIZEN[1]

*On August 27, 1789, the French Constituent Assembly adopted their famous declaration. It reflected the aspirations of the middle classes who wanted an end to aristocratic privilege but whose concept of human rights did not include economic and social rights for the lower classes.*

γ        γ        γ

The representatives of the people of France, formed into a National Assembly, considering that ignorance, neglect, or contempt of human rights, are the sole causes of public misfortunes and corruptions of government, have resolved to set forth in a solemn declaration, these natural, imprescriptible, and inalienable rights: that this declaration being constantly present to the minds of the members of the body social, they may be forever kept attentive to their rights and duties; that the acts of the legislative and executive powers of government, being capable of being every moment compared with the end of political institutions, may be more respected; and also, that the future claims of the citizens, being directed by simple and incontestable principles, may always tend to the maintenance of the Constituion, and the general happiness.

For these reasons, the National Assembly doth recognize and declare, in the presence of the Supreme Being, and with the hope of His blessing and favor, the following *sacred* rights of men and citizens:

I.    Men are born, and always continue, free and equal in respect of their rights. Civil distinctions, therefore, can be founded only on public utility.

[1] Leo Gershoy, *The Era of the French Revolution* (Princeton, 1957), Anvil No. 22, translation from the French by Leo Gershoy. Courtesy of Leo Gershoy estate.

II.   The end of all political associations is the preservation of the natural and imprescriptible rights of man; and these rights are liberty, property, security, and resistance of oppression.

III. The nation is essentially the source of all sovereignty; nor can any individual, or any body of men, be entitled to any authority which is not expressly derived from it.

IV. Political liberty consists in the power of doing whatever does not injure another. The exercise of the natural rights of every man, has no other limits than those which are necessary to secure to every *other* man the free exercise of the same rights; and these limits are determinable only by law.

V.   The law ought to prohibit only actions hurtful to society. What is not prohibited by the law, should not be hindered; nor should anyone be compelled to that which the law does not require.

VI. The law is an expression of the will of the community. All citizens have a right to concur, either personally, or by their representatives, in its formation. It should be the same to all, whether it protects or punishes; and all being equal in its sight, are equally eligible to all honors, places, and employments, according to their different abilities, without any other distinction than that created by their virtues and talents.

VII. No man should be accused, arrested, or held in confinement, except in cases determined by the law, and according to the forms which it has prescribed.

VIII. The law ought to impose no other penalties but such as are absolutely and evidently necessary; and no one ought to be punished, but in virtue of a law promulgated before the offense, and legally applied.

IX. Every man being presumed innocent till he has been convicted, whenever his detention becomes indispensable, all rigor to him, more than is necessary to secure his person, ought to be provided against by the law.

X.   No man ought to be molested on account of his opinions, not even on account of his *religious* opinions, provided his avowal of them does not distrub the public order established by the law.

XI.   The unrestrained communication of thoughts and opinions being one of the most precious rights of man, every citizen may speak, write, and publish freely, provided he is responsible for the abuse of this liberty, in cases determined by the law.

XII.   A public force being necessary to give security to the rights of men and of citizens, that force is instituted for the benefit of the community and not for the particular benefit of the persons to whom it is intrusted.

XIII.   A common contribution being necessary for the support of the public force, and for defraying to other expenses of government, it ought to be divided equally among the members of the community, according to their abilities.

XIV.   Every citizen has a right, either by himself or his representative, to a free voice in determining the necessity of public contributions, the appropriation of them, and their amount, mode of assessment, and duration.

XV.   Every community has a right to demand of all its agents an account of their conduct.

XVI.   Every community in which a separation of powers and a security of rights is not provided for, wants a consititution.

XVII.   The right to property being inviolable and sacred, no one ought to be deprived of it, except in cases of evident public necessity, legally ascertained, and on condition of a previous just indemnity.

\#                    \#

# BENTHAM: NATURAL RIGHTS A FALLACY[2]

*In the following passage Jeremy Bentham asserts his belief that the basis for any right is its utility to society and not its dependence on natural law. He argues that the concept of natural rights limits freedom rather than expanding it.*

γ       γ       γ

In proportion to the want of happiness resulting from the want of rights, a reason exists for wishing that there were such things as rights. But reasons for wishing there were such things as rights, are not rights;—a reason for wishing that a certain right were established, is not that right—want is not supply—hunger is not bread.

That which has no existence cannot be destoryed—that which cannot be destoryed cannot require anything to preserve it from destruction *Natural rights* is simple nonsense: natural and imprescriptible rights, rhetroical nonsense,—nonsense upon stilts. But this rhetorical nonsense ends in the old strain of mischievous nonsense: for immediately a list of these pretended natural rights is given, and those are so expressed to present to view legal rights. And of these rights, whatever they are, there is not, it seems, any one of which any government *can*, upon any occasion whatever, abrogate the smallest particle.

So much for terrorist language. What is the language of reason and plain sense upon this same subject? That in proportion as it is *right* or *proper*, i.e. advantageous to the society in question, that this or that right—a right to this or that effect—should be established and maintained, in that same proportion it is *wrong* that it should be abrogated: but that as there is no *right*, which ought not to be maintained so long as it is upon the whole advantageous to the society that it should be maintained, so

[2] Jeremy Bentham, *Works,* ed. John Bowring (London, 1843), vol. II, pp. 107-111.

there is no right which, when the abolition of it is advantageous to society, should not be abolished. To know whether it would be more for the advantage of society that this or that right should be maintained or abolished, the time at which the question about maintaining or abolishing is proposed, must be given the circumstances under which it is proposed to maintain or abolish it; the right itself must be specifically described, not jumbled with an undistinguishable heap of others, under any such vague general terms as property, liberty, and the like.

One thing, in the midst of all this confusion, is but too plain. They know not of what they are talking under the name of natural rights, and yet they would have them imprescriptible—proof against all the power of the laws—pregnant with occasions summoning the member of the community to rise up in resistance against the laws. What, then, was their object in declaring the existence of imprescriptible rights, and without specifying a single one by any such mark as it could be known by? This and no other—to excite and keep up a spirit of resistance to all laws— a spirit of insurrection against all governments—against the governments of all other nations instantly,—against the government of their own nation—against the government they themselves were pretending to establish—even that, as soon as their own reign should be at an end. In us is the perfection of virtue and wisdom: in all mankind besides, the extremity of wickedness and folly. Our will shall consequently reign without control, and for ever: reign now we are living—reign after we are dead.

All nations—all future ages—shall be, for they are predestined to be, our slaves.

Future governments will not have honestly enough to be trusted with the determination of what rights shall be maintained, what abrogated—what laws kept in force, what repealed. Future subjects (I should say future citizens, for French government does not admit of subjects) will not have wit enough to be trusted with the choice whether to submit to the determination of the government of their time, or resist it. Governments, citizens—all to the end of time—all must be kept in chains.

Such are their maxims—such their premises—for it is by such premises only that the doctrine of imprescriptible rights and unrepealable laws can be supported.

What is the real source of these imprescriptible rights—these unrepealable laws? Power turned blind by looking from its own height: self-conceit and tyranny exalted into insanity. No man was to have any other man for a servant, yet all men were forever to be their slaves. Making laws with imposture in their mouths, under pretence of declaring them—giving for laws anything that came uppermost, and these unrepealable ones, on pretence of finding them ready made. Made by what? Not by a God—they allow of none; but by their goddess, Nature.

The origination of governments from a contract is a pure fiction, or in other words, a falsehood. It never has been known to be true in any instance; the allegation of it does mischief, by involving the subject in error and confusion, and is neither necessary nor useful to any good purpose.

All governments that we have any account of have been gradually established by habit, after having been formed by force; unless in the instance of governments formed by individuals who have been emancipated, or have emancipated themselves, from governments already formed, the governments under which they were born—a rare case, and from which nothing follows with regard to the rest. What signifies it how governments are formed? Is it the less proper—the less conducive to the happiness of society—that the happiness of society should be the one object kept in view by the members of the government in all their measures? Is it the less the interest of men to be happy—less to be wished that they may be so—less the moral duty of their governors to make them so, as far as they can, at Mogadore than at Philadelphia?

Whence is it, but from government, that contracts derive their binding force? Contracts came from government, not government from contracts. It is from the habit of enforcing contracts, and seeing them enforced, that governments are chiefly indebted for whatever disposition they have to observe them.

#                    #

## UNIVERSAL DECLARATION OF HUMAN RIGHTS[3]

*On December 10, 1948, the General Assembly of the United Nations adopted and proclaimed the Universal Declaration of Human Rights. Although its provision are observed in few countries, it represents the best modern standard of human rights. The following extracts constitute its chief provision.*

γ　　　　γ　　　　γ

### THE GENERAL ASSEMLBY

*proclaims*

THIS UNIVERSAL DECLARATION OF HUMAN RIGHTS as a common standard of achievement for all peoples and all nations, to the end that every individual and every organ of society, keeping this Declaration constantly in mind, shall strive by teaching and education to promote respect for these rights and freedoms and by progressive measures, national and international, to secure their universal and effectve recognition and observance, both among the peoples of Member States themselves and among the peoples of territories under their jurisdiction.

All human beings are born free and equal in dignity and rights. They are endowed with reason and conscience and should act towards one another in a spirit of brotherhood.

Everyone is entitled to all the rights and freedoms set forth in this Declaration, without distinction of any kind, such as race, colour, sex, language, religion, political or other opinion, national or social origin, property, birth or other status. Furthermore, no distinction shall be made on the basis of the political, jurisdictional or international status of the country or territory to which a person belongs, whether it be independent, trust, non-self-governing or under any other limitation of sovereignty.

[3]Courtesy of the United Nations.

Everyone has the right to life, liberty and security of person. . . .

No one shall be subjected to torture or cruel, inhuman or degrading treatment or punishment. . . .

All are equal before the law and are entitled without any discrimination to equal protection of the law. All are entitled to equal protection against any discrimination in violation of this Declaration and against any incitement to such discrimination. . . .

No one shall be subjected to arbitrary arrest, detention or exile. . . .

Everyone charged with a penal offence has the right to be presumed innocent until proved guilty according to law in a public trial at which he has had all the guarantees necessary for his defense. . . .

No one shall be subjected to arbitrary interference with his privacy, family, home, or correspondence, nor to attacks upon his honor or reputation. Everyone has the right to the protection of the law against such interference or attacks.

Everyone has the right to freedom of movement and residence within the borders of each state.

Everyone has the right to leave any country, including his own, and return to his country.

Everyone has the right to seek and to enjoy in other countries asylum from persecution. . . .

Everyone has the right to a nationality.

No one shall be arbitrarily deprived of his nationality nor denied the right to change his nationality.

Men and women of full age, without any limitation due to race, nationality or religion, have the right to marry and to found a family. They are entitled to equal rights as to marriage, during marriage and at its dissolution.

Marriage shall be entered into only with the free and full consent of the intending spouses.

The family is the natural and fundamental group unit of society and is entitled to protection by society and the State. . . .

Everyone has the right to freedom of thought, conscience and religion; this right includes freedom to change his religion or belief, and freedom, either alone or in community with others and in public or private, to mainifest his religion or belief in teaching, practice, worship and observance.

Everyone has the right to freedom of opinion and expression; this right includes freedom to hold opinions without interference and to seek, receive and impart information and ideas through any media and regardless of frontiers.

Everyone has the right to freedom of peaceful assembly and association.

Everyone has the right to take part in the government of his country, directly or through freely chosen representatives.

Everyone has the right of equal access to public service in his country.

The will of the people shall be the basis of the authority of government; this will shall be expressed in periodic and genuine elections which shall be by universal and equal suffrage and shall be held by secret vote or by equivalent free voting procedures.

Everyone, as a member of society, has the right to social security and is entitled to realisation, through national effort and international co-operation and in accordance with the organisation and resources of each State, of the economic, social and cultural rights indispensable for his dignity and the free development of his personality.

Everyone has the right to work, to free choice of employment, to just and favourable conditions of work and to protection against unemployment.

Everyone, without any discrimination, has the right to equal pay for equal work.

Everyone who works has the right to just and favourable remuneration insuring for himself and his family an existence worthy of human dignity, and supplemented, if necessary by other means of social protection.

Everyone has the right to form and to join trade unions for the protection of his interests.

Everyone has the right to rest and leisure, including reasonable limitation of working hours and periodic holidays with pay.

Everyone has the right to a standard of living adequate for the health and well-being of himself and of his family, including food, clothing, housing and medical care and necessary social services, and the right to security in the event of unemployment, sickness, disability, widowhood, old age or other lack of livelihood in circumstances beyond his control.

Motherhood and childhood are entitled to special care and assistance. All children whether born in or out of wedlock, shall enjoy the same social protection.

Everyone has the right to education. Education shall be free, at least in the elementary and fundamental stages. Elemementary education shall be compulsory. Technical and professional education shall be made generally available and higher education shall be equally accessible to all on the basis of merit. . . .

Everyone has the right freely to participate in the cultural life of the community, to enjoy the arts and to share in scientific advancement and its benefits. . . .

Everyone has duties to the community in which alone the free and full development of his personality is possible . . . .

Nothing in this Declaration may be interpreted as implying for any State, group or person any right to engage in any activity or to perform any act aimed at the destruction of any of the rights and freedoms set forth herein.

#          #

# CICERO: BROTHERHOOD OF MAN[4]

*An important political figure in the age of Julius Caesar, Marcus Tullius Cicero wrote numerous treatises of law. Cicero believed in a universal natural law that "will not lay down one rule at Rome and another at Athens nor will it be one rule today and another tomorrow." One of the chief bases of this natural law was the equality of all men.*

γ        γ        γ

And so however we may define man, a single definition will apply to all. This is sufficient proof that there is no difference in kind between man and man; for if there were, one definition could not be applicable to all men; and indeed reason which alone raises us above the level of the beasts and enables us to draw inferences, to prove and disprove, to discuss and solve problems, and to come to conclusions is certainly common to us all and though varying in what it learns, at least in the capacity to learn it is invariable. For the same things are invariably perceived by the senses and those things which stimulate the senses, stimulate them in the same way in all men and those rudimentary beginnings of intelligence to which I referred, which are imprinted on our minds, are imprinted on all minds alike; and speech the mind's interpreter though differing the the choice of words, agrees in the sentiments expressed. In fact there is no human being of any race who if he finds a guide cannot attain a virtue.

\#             \#

[4] Marcus Tullius Cicero, *De republica de legibus* (New York, 1928), p. 109. Trans. by Clinton Walker Keyes.

## THE SERMON ON THE MOUNT[5]

*In the Sermon on the mount, Jesus traces the living law of his new kingdom. He outlines the character of the Christian life. The moral philosophy outlined in the Sermon is a gauntlet flung down before the world's accepted standards.*

γ         γ         γ

"Blessed are the poor in spirit, for theirs is the kingdom of heaven.

"Blessed are those who mourn, for they shall be comforted.

"Blessed are the meek, for they shall inherit the earth.

"Blessed are those who hunger and thirst for righteousness, for they shall be satisfied.

"Blessed are the merciful, for they shall obtain mercy.

"Blessed are the pure in heart, for they shall see God.

"Blessed are the peacemakers, for they shall be called sons of God.

"Blessed are those who are persecuted for righteousness' sake, for theirs is the kingdom of heaven.

"Blessed are you when men revile you and persecute you and utter all kinds of evil against you falsely on my account. Rejoice and be glad, for your reward is great in heaven, for so men persecuted the prophets who were before you.

#         #

[5]*Matthew* 5:1-12.

## THE MAGNA CHARTA[6]

*The Magna Charta was reissued several times after 1215 with various changes. The reissue of 1225 became the official version of succeeding monarchs. It was annulled within three months by Pope Innocent III, but he could not defeat the concept that a king was bound by law. The Magna Charta's greatest contributions to human rights were to develop over the course of centuries. "Freeman" in Article 39 originally referred to a baron but it gradually evolved that the document referred to fundamental rights for all the people and not one class.*

γ γ γ

1. First of all have granted to God, and, for us and for our heirs forever, have confirmed, by this our present charter, that the English church shall be free and shall have its rights intact and its liberties uninfringed upon. And thus we will that it be observed. As is apparent from the fact that we, spontaneously and of our own free will, before discord broke out between ourselves and our barons, did grant and by our charter confirm—and did cause the lord pope Innocent III to confirm—freedom of elections, which is considered most important and most necessary to the church of England. Which charter both we ourselves shall observe, and we will that it be observed with good faith by our heirs forever. We have also granted to all free men of our realm, on the part of ourselves and our heirs forever, all the subjoined liberties, to have and to hold, to them and to their heirs, from us and from our heirs. . . .

9. Neither we nor our bailiffs shall seize any revenue for any debt, so long as the chattels of the debtor suffice to pay the debt; nor shall the sponsors of that debtor be distrained so long as the chief debtor has enough to pay

[6] E.F. Henderson, *Historical Documents of the Middle Ages* (London, 1896), pp. 135-148.

the debt. But if the chief debtor fail in paying the debt, not having the wherewithal to pay it, the sponsors shall answer for the debt. And, if they shall wish, they may have the lands and revenues of the debtor until satisfaction shall have been given them for the debt previously paid for him; unless the chief debtor shall show that he is quit in that respect towards those same sponsors. . . .

12. No scuttage or aid shall be imposed in our realm unless by the common counsel of our realm; except for redeeming our body, and knighting our eldest son, and marrying once our eldest daughter. And for these purposes there shall only be given a reasonable aid. In like manner shall be done concerning the aids of the city of London.

13. And the city of London shall have all its old liberties and free customs as well by land as by water. Moreover we will and grant that all other cities and burroughs, and towns and ports, shall have all their liberties and free customs.

14. And, in order to have the common cousel of the realm in the matter of assessing an aid otherwise than in the aforesaid cases, or of assessing a scutage,—we shall cause, under seal through our letters, the archbishops, bishops, abbots, earls, and greater barons to be summoned for a fixed day—for a term, namely, at least forty days distant,—and for a fixed place. And, moreover, we shall cause to be summoned in general, through our sheriffs and bailiffs, all those who hold of us in chief. And in all those letters of summons we shall express the cause of the summons. And when a summons has thus been made, the business shall be proceeded with on the day appointed according to the counsel of those who shall be present, even though not all shall come who were summoned.

15. We will not allow anyone henceforth to take an aid from his freemen save for the redemption of his body, and the knighting of his eldest son, and the marrying, once, of his eldest daughter; and, for these purposes, there shall only be given a reasonable aid.

16. No one shall be forced to do more service for a knight's fee, or for another free holding, than is due from it.

17. Common pleas shall not follow our court but shall be held in a certain fixed place.

38. No bailiff, on his own simple assertion, shall henceforth put anyone to his law, without producing faithful witnesses in evidence.

39. No freeman shall be taken, or imprisoned, or diseized, or outlawed, or exiled, or in any way harmed—nor will we go upon or send upon him—save by the lawful judgment of his peers or by the law of the land.

40. To none will we sell, to none deny or delay, right or justice. . . .

45. We will not make men justices, constables, sheriffs, or bailiffs, unless they are such as know the law of the realm, and are minded to observe it rightly. . . .

63. Wherefore we will and firmly decree that the English church shall be free, and that the subjects of our realm shall have and hold all the aforesaid liberties, rights and concessions, duly and in peace, freely and quietly, fully and entirely, for themselves and their heirs, from us and our heirs, in all matters and in all places, forever, as has been said. Moreover it has been sworn, on our part as well as on the part of the barons, that all these above mentioned provisions shall be observed with good faith and without evil intent. The witnesses being the above mentioned and many others. Given through our hand, in the plain called Runnimede between Windsor and Stanes, on the fifteenth day of June, in the seventeenth year of our reign.

#          #

## LOCKE: RIGHT OF REVOLUTION[7]

*John Locke was a major figure in the history of human freedom. In his* Letter *on* Toleration, *he forcibly argued that no government can give to the Church power to limit the religious observance of its citizens. In the following excerpt, he argues that government can only rule with the consent of the governed.*

γ           γ           γ

Men being, as has been said, by nature all free, equal, and independent, no one can be put out of this estate and subjected to the political power of another without his own consent, which is done by agreeing with other men, to join and unite into a community for their comfortable, safe, and peaceable living, one amongst another, in a secure enjoyment of their properties, and a greater security against any that are not of it. This any number of men may do, because it injures not the freedom of the rest; they are left, as they were, in the liberty of the state of Nature. When any number of men have so consented to make one community or government, they are thereby presently incorporated, and make one body politic, wherein the majority have a right to act and conclude the rest.

For, when any number of men have, by the consent of every individual, made a community, they have thereby made that community one body, with a power to act as one body, which is only by the will and determination of the majority. For that which acts any community, being only the consent of the individuals of it, and it being one body, must move one way, it is necessary the body should move that way whither the greater force carries it, which is the consent of the majority, or else it is impossible it

[7] John Locke, *Of Civil Government* (New York, 1924), pp. 164-165, 219, 228-229.

should act or continue one body, one community, which the consent of every individual that united onto it agreed that it should; and so every one is bound by that consent to be concluded by the majority. And therefore we see that in assemblies empowered to act by positive laws where no number is set by that positive law which empowers them, the act of the majority passes for the act of the whole, and of course determines as having, by the law of Nature and reason, the power of the whole. . . .

Wherever law ends, tyranny begins, if the law be transgressed to another's harm; and whosoever in authority exceeds the power given him by the law, and makes use of the force he has under his command to compass that upon the subject which the law allows not, ceases in that to be a magistrate, and acting without authority may be opposed, as any other man who by force invades the right of another.

. . . For since it can never be supposed to be the will of society that the legislative should have a power to destroy that which every one designs to secure by entering into society, and for which the people submitted themselves to legislators of their own making: whenever the legislators endeavor to take away and destroy the property of the people, or to reduce them to slavery under arbitrary power, they put themselves into a state of war with the people, who are thereupon absolved from any farther obedience, and are left to the common refuge which God hath provided for all men against force and violence. Whensoever, therefore, the legislative shall transgress this fundamental rule of society, . . . it devolves to the people, who have a right to resume their original liberty, and by the establishment of a new legislature (such as they shall think fit) provide for their own safety and security, which is the end for which they are in society. What I have said here concerning the legislative in general holds true also concerning the supreme executor, . . . when he goes about to set up his own arbitrary will as the law of society.

#          #          #

## THE ENGLISH BILL OF RIGHTS[8]

*Before William and Mary were allowed to take the throne in 1689, they were obliged to sign a Declaration which has become the English Bill of Rights. More than any other document, it is the fundamental basis of England's unwritten Constitution. The Bill of Rights offers a comprehensive restatement of the principles of English freedom as set forth in Magna Charta.*

γ     γ     γ

Whereas the said late King James II having abdicated the government, and the throne being thereby vacant, his Highness the prince of Orange . . . (by the advice of the Lords spiritual and temporal, and divers principal persons of the Commons) . . . being now assembled in a full and free representative of this nation, taking into their most serious consideration the best means for attaining the ends aforesaid, do in the first place (as their ancestors in like case have usually done), for the vindicating and asserting their ancient rights and liberties, declare:

1. That the pretended power of suspending laws, or the execution of laws, by regal authority, without consent of Parliament, is illegal.

2. That the pretended power of dispensing with laws, or the execution of laws, by regal authority, as it has been assumed and exercised of late, is illegal.

3. That the commission for erecting the late Court of Commissioners for Ecclesiastical Causes, and all other commissions and courts of like nature, are illegal and pernicious.

[8]R.P. Stearns (ed.), *Pageant of Europe* (New York, 1948), pp. 235-237.

4. That levying money for or to the use of the crown, by pretence of prerogative, without grant of Parliament, for longer time, or in other manner than the same is or shall be granted, is illegal.

5. That it is the right of the subjects to petition the king, and all commitments and prosecutions for such petitioning are illegal.

6. That the raising or keeping a standing army within the kingdom in time of peace, unless it be with consent of Parliament, is against law.

7. That the subjects which are Protestants may have arms for their defence suitable to their conditions, and as allowed by law.

8. That election of members of Parliament ought to be free.

9. That the freedom of speech, and debates or proceedings in Parliament, ought not to be impeached or questioned in any court or place out of Parliament.

10. That excessive bail ought not to be required, nor excessive fines imposed, nor cruel and unusual punishments inflicted.

11. That jurors ought to be duly impaneled and returned, and jurors which pass upon men in trials for high treason ought to be freeholders.

12. That all grants and promises of fines and forfeitures of particular persons before conviction are illegal and void.

13. And that for redress of all grievances, and for the amending, strengthening, and preserving of the laws, Parliament ought to be held frequently.

And they do claim, demand, and insist upon all and singular the premises, as their undoubted rights and liberties; and that no declarations, judgments, doings, or proceedings, to the prejudice of the people in any of the said premises, ought in any wise to be drawn hereafter into consequence or example. . . .

#          #

## MILTON: CENSORSHIP[9]

*Aeropagitica, written by John Milton in 1644, remains as a classic expression of the freedom of conscience. Ironically, perhaps because Milton used a style which was too intellecutal and scholarly, his tract lacked popular appeal.* Aeropagitica *was little noticed at the time but has been greatly appreciated by later generations.*

γ       γ       γ

I deny not, but that it is of greatest concernment in the church and commonwealth, to have a vigilant eye how books demean themselves, as well as men; and thereafter to confine, imprison, and do sharpest justice on them as malefactors; for books are not absolutely dead things, but do contain a progeny of life in them to be as active as that soul was whose progeny they are; nay, they do preserve as in a vial the purest efficacy and extraction of that living intellect that bred them. I know they are as lively, and as vigorously productive, as those fabulous dragon's teeth: and being sown up and down, may chance to spring up armed men. And yet, on the other hand, unless wariness be used, as good almost kill a man as kill a good book: who kills a man kills a reasonable creature, God's image; but he who destroys a good book, kills reason itself, kills the image of God, as it were, in the eye. Many a man lives a burthen to the earth; but a good book is the precious lifeblood of a master-spirit, embalmed and treasured up on purpose to a life beyond life . . .

We should be wary, therefore, what persecution we raise against the living labours of public men, how we spill that reasoned life of man, preserved and stored up in

[9] John Milton, *Aeropagitica and other Prose Writings,* ed. William Haller (New York, 1927), pp. 809.

books; since we see a kind of homicide may be thus committed, sometimes a martyrdom; and if it extend to the whole impression, a kind of massacre, whereof the execution ends not in the slaying of an elemental life, but strikes at the ethereal and fifth essence, the breath of reason itself, slays an immortality rather than a life.

#        #

# ROGER WILLIAMS: FREEDOM OF RELIGION[10]

*Roger Williams founded Rhode Island as "a shelter for persons distressed of conscience" where everyone professing any kind of Christian belief could have the full enjoyment of political rights "as long as he does not violate peace and quietness and does not abuse this liberty in a licentious and profane manner." Later, Jews were admitted to the rights of citizenship. The following passage is an impassioned plea by Williams for religious toleration.*

γ　　　　γ　　　　γ

I acknowledge that to harm any person Jew or Gentile for either professing doctrine or practicing worship . . . is to persecute him and such a person (whether his doctrine or practice be true or false) suffers persecution for conscience. . . . Breach of civil peace may arise when false and idolatrous practices are held, but from that wrong and preposterous way of suppressing, preventing or extinguishing such doctrines or practices by weapons of wrath and blood, whips, stocks, imprisonment, death, etc., by which men commonly are persuaded to convert heretics and to cast out unclean spirits which only the finger of God can do, that is the mighty power of the spirit in the Word.

Hence the town is in an uproar and the country takes the alarm to expel that fog of mist of error heresy, blasphemy (as is supposed) with swords and guns, whereas it is a light alone, from the bright shining Sun of Righteousness, which is able in the souls and conscience of men to dispel and scatter such fogs and darkness.

#　　　　#

[10] Roger Williams, *The Bloody Tenets of Persecution* (Providence, R.I., 1867), pp. 38-39. The style modernized here.

## THE VIRGINIA DECLARATION OF RIGHTS[11]

*The document adopted in Virginia on June 12, 1776, was a ringing affirmation of certain inherent rights including freedom of press, trial by jury, separation of powers, and, most importantly, religious toleration. This latter right became definite when the Statute of Religious Liberty, drawn up by Thomas Jefferson, was passed by The Virginia legislature in 1786.*

γ   γ   γ

A declaration of rights, made by the Representatives of the good People of Virginia, assembled in full and free Convention, which rights do pertain to them and their posterity as the basis and foundation of government.

I. That all men are by nature equally free and independent, and have certain inherent rights, of which, when they enter into a state of society, they cannot by any compact deprive or divest their posterity; namely, the enjoyment of life and liberty, with the means of acquiring and possessing property, and pursuing and obtaining happiness and safety.

II. That all power is vested in, and consequently derived from, the people; that magistrates are their trustees and servants, and at all times amenable to them.

III. That government is, or ought to be, instituted for the common benefit, protection, and security of the people, nation or community; of all the various modes and forms of government, that is best which is capable of producing the greatest degree of happiness and safety, and is most effectually secured against the danger of maladministration; and that, when a government shall be found inadequate or contrary to these purposes, a

[11] From the official text.

majority of the community hath an indubitable, unalienable, and indefeasible right to reform, alter or abolish it, in such manner as shall be judged most conducive to the public weal.

IV. That no man, or set of men, are entitled to exclusive or separate emoluments of privileges from the community but in consideration of public services, which not being descendible, neither ought the offices of magistrate, legislator or judge to be hereditary.

V. That the legislative, executive and judicial powers should be separate and distinct; and that the members thereof may be restrained from oppression, by feeling and participating the burthens of the people, they should, at fixed periods, be reduced to a private station, return into that body from which they were originally taken, and the vacancies be supplied by frequent, certain and regular elections, in which all, or any part of the former members to be again eligible or ineligible, as the laws shall direct.

VI. That all elections ought to be free, and that all men having sufficient evidence of permanent common interest with, and attachment to the community, have the right of suffrage, and cannot be taxed, or deprived of their property for public uses, without their own consent, or that of their representatives so elected, nor bound by any law to which they have not in like manner assented, for the public good.

VII. That all power of suspending laws, or the execution of laws, by any authority, without consent of the representatives of the people, is injurious to their rights, and ought not to be exercised.

VIII. That in all capital or criminal prosecutions a man hath a right to demand the cause and nature of his accusation, to be confronted with the accusers and witnesses, to call for evidence in his favour, and to a speedy trial by an impartial jury of twelve men of his vicinage, without whose unanimous consent he cannot be found guilty; nor can he be compelled to give evidence against himself; that no man be deprived of this liberty, except by the law of the land or the judgment of his peers.

IX. That excessive bail ought not to be required, nor excessive fines imposed, nor cruel and unusual punishments inflicted.

X. That general warrants, whereby an officer or messenger may be commanded to search suspected places without evidence of a fact committed, or to seize any person or persons not named, or whose offence is not particularly described and supported by evidence, are grievous and oppressive, and ought not to be granted.

XI. That in controversies respecting property, and in suits between man and man, the ancient trial by jury of twelve men is preferable to any other, and ought to be held sacred.

XII. That the freedom of the press is one of the great bulwarks of liberty, and can never be restrained but by despotic governments.

XIII. That a well-regulated militia, composed of the body of the people, trained to arms, is the proper, natural and safe defence of a free State: that standing armies in time of peace should be avoided as dangerous to liberty; and that in all cases the military should be under strict subordination to, and governed by, the civil power.

XIV. That the people have a right to uniform government; and therefore that no government separate from or independent of the government of Virginia ought to be erected or established within the limits thereof.

XV. That no free government, or the blessing of liberty, can be preserved to any people, but by a firm adherence to justice, moderation, temperance, frugality and virtue, and by a frequent recurrence to fundamental principles.

XVI. That religion, or the duty which we owe to our Creator, and the manner of discharging it, can be directed only by reason and conviction, not by force or violence; and therefore all men are equally entitled to the free exercise of religion, according to the dictates of conscience; and that it is the duty of all to practice Christian forbearance, love and charity towards each other.

\#                              \#

## THE DECLARATION OF INDEPENDENCE [12]

*On July 4, 1776, the Declaration of Independence was adopted by the Continental Congress. The first two paragraphs reflect a belief in a concept of human rights based on natural law.*

γ       γ       γ

When in the Course of human events, it becomes necessary for one people to dissolve the political bands which have connected them with another, and to assume among the powers of the earth, the separate and equal station to which the Laws of Nature and of Nature's God entitle them, a decent respect to the opinions of mankind requires that they should declare the causes which impel them to the separation.

We hold these truths to be self-evident, that all men are created equal, that they are endowed by their Creator with certain unalienable Rights, that among these are Life, Liberty and the pursuit of Happiness.—That to secure these rights, Governments are instituted among Men, deriving their just powers from the consent of the governed—That whenever any Form of Government becomes destructive of these ends, it is the Right of the People to alter or abolish it, and to institute new Government, laying its foundation on such principles and organizing its powers in such form, as to them shall seem most likely to effect their Safety and Happiness. Prudence, indeed, will dictate that Governments long established should not be changed for light and transient causes; and accordingly all experience hath shewn, that mankind are more disposed to suffer, while evils are sufferable, than to right themselves by abolishing the forms to which they are accustomed. But when a long train of abuses and usurpations,

[12] The official text.

pursuing invariably the same Object evinces a design to reduce them under absolute Despotism, it is their right, it is their duty, to throw off such Government, and to provide new Guards for their future security.—Such has been the patient sufferance of these Colonies; and such is now the necessity which constrains them to alter their former Systems of Government. The history of the present King of Great Britain is a history of repeated injuries and usurpations, all having in direct object the establishment of an absolute Tyranny over these States. To prove this, let Facts be submitted to a candid world.

#                    #

## THE AMERICAN BILL OF RIGHTS [13]

*After the adoption of the Constitution, George Mason was the leader of a thoughtful group of political leaders who believed that a specific Bill of Rights was necessary. On June 8, 1789, James Madison, the Father of the Constitution, spoke in Congress in favor of a Bill of Rights. On December 15, 1791, the Bill of Rights became part of the Constitution.*

γ          γ          γ

1. Congress shall make no law respecting an establishment of religion, or prohibiting the free exercise thereof; or abridging the freedom of speech, or of the press; or the right of the people peaceably to assemble, and to petition the government for a redress of grievances.

2. A well-regulated militia being necessary to the security of a free state, the right of the people to keep and bear arms shall not be infringed.

3. No soldier shall, in time of peace, be quartered in any house, without the consent of the owner; nor in time of war, but in a manner to be prescribed by law.

4. The right of the people to be secure in their persons, houses, papers, and effects, against unreasonable searches and seizures, shall not be violated; and no warrants shall issue, but upon probable cause, supported by oath or affirmation, and particularly describing the place to be searched, and the persons or things to be seized.

5. No person shall be held to answer for a capital or other infamous crime unless on a presentment or indictment of a Grand Jury, except in cases arising in the land or naval forces, or in the militia, when in actual service, in time of war or public danger; nor shall any person be subject, for the same offense, to be twice put in jeopardy of life or limb; nor shall be compelled, in any criminal case, to be a witness against himself; nor be deprived of

[13] The official text.

life, liberty, or property, without due process of law; nor shall private property be taken for public use, without just compensation.

6. In all criminal prosecutions, the accused shall enjoy the right to a speedy and public trial, by an impartial jury of the state and district wherein the crime shall have been committed, which district shall have been previously ascertained by law, and to be informed of the nature and cause of the accusation; to be confronted with the witnesses against him; to have compulsory process for obtaining witnesses in his favor, and to have the assistance of counsel for his defense.

7. In suits at common law, where the value in controversy shall exceed twenty dollars, the right of trial by jury shall be preserved, and no fact tried by a jury shall be otherwise re-examined in any court of the United States than according to the rules of the common law.

8. Excessive bail shall not be required, nor excessive fines imposed, nor cruel and unusual punishments inflicted.

9. The enumeration in the Constitution of certain rights shall not be construed to deny or disparage others retained by the people.

10. The powers not delegated to the United States by the Constitution, nor prohibited by it to the states, are reserved to the states respectively, or to the people.

#          #

## BURKE: RIGHTS DERIVED FROM TRADITION[14]

*Edmund Bruke based his critique of the French Revolution on ideas which he developed during his long struggle against parliamentary reform in Great Britain, In the following passage, he asserts his belief that societies must change, if at all, by an imperceptible organic growth; custom, tradition, and habit must determine the content of law.*

γ          γ

You will observe, that from Magna Charta to the Declaration of Right, it has been the uniform policy of our constitution to claim and assert our liberties, as an entailed inheritance derived to us from our forefathers and to be transmitted to our posterity; as an estate specially belonging to the people of this kingdom, without any reference whatever to any other more general or prior right. By this means our constitution preserves a unity in so great a diversity of its parts. We have an inheritable crown; an inheritable peerage; and a House of Commons and a people inheriting privileges, franchises, and liberties, from a long line of ancestors.

This policy appears to me to be the result of profound reflection; of rather the happy effect of following nature, which is wisdom without reflection, and above it. A spirit of innovation is generally the result of a selfish temper, and confined views. People will not look forward to posterity, who never look backward to their ancestors. Besides, the people of England well know, that the idea of inheritance furnishes a sure principle of conservation, and a sure principle of transmission, without at all excluding a principle of improvement. It leaves acquisition free; but

[14]Edmund Burke, *Works of Edmund Burke* (London, 1872-1873), vol. II, pp. 306-309.

it secures what it acquires. Whatever advantages are obtained by a state proceeding on these maxims, are locked fast as in a sort of family settlement; grasped as in a kind of mortmain for ever. By a constitutional policy, working after the pattern of nature, we receive, we hold, we transmit our government and our privileges, in the same manner in which we enjoy and transmit our property and our lives. The institutions of policy, the goods of fortune, the gifts of providence, are handed down to us, and from us, in the same course and order. Our political system is placed in a just correspondence and symmetry with the order of the world, and with the mode of existence decreed to a permanent body composed of transitory parts; wherein by the disposition of a stupendous wisdom, moulding together the great mysterious incorporation of the human race, the whole, at one time, is never old, or middle-aged, or young, but, in a condition of unchangeable constancy, moves on through the varied tenor of perpetual decay, fall, renovation, and progression. Thus, by preserving the method of nature in the conduct of the state, in what we improve, we are never wholly new; in what we retain, we are never wholly obsolete. By adhering in this manner and on those principles to our forefathers, we are guided not by the superstition of antiquarians, but by the spirit of philosophic analogy. In this choice of inheritence we have given to our frame of polity the image of a relation in blood; binding up the constitution of our country with our dearest domestic ties; adopting our fundamental laws into the bosom of our family affections; keeping inseparable, and cherishing with the warmth of all their combined and mutually reflected charities, our state, our hearths, our sepulchres, and our altars.

Through the same plan of a conformity to nature in our artifical institutions, and by calling in the aid of her unerring and powerful instincts, to fortify the fallible and feeble contrivances of our reason, we have derived several other, and those no small benefits, from considering our liberties in the light of an inheritance. Always acting as if in the presence of canonized forefathers, the spirit of freedom, leading in itself to misrule and excess, is tempered with an awful gravity. This idea of a liberal descent inspires us with a sense of habitual native dignity, which prevents that upstart insolence almost inevitably adhering to and disgracing those who are the first acquirers of any distinction. By this means our liberty becomes a noble freedom. It carries an imposing and majestic aspect. It has a pedigree and illustrating ancestors. It has its bearings and its ensigns armorial. It has its gallery of portraits; its monumental inscriptions; its records, evidences, and titles. We procure reference to our civil institutions on the principle upon which nature teaches us to revere individual men; on account of their age, and on account of those from whom they are descended. All your sophisters cannot produce anything better adapted to preserve a rational and manly freedom than the course that we have pursued, who have chosen our nature rather than our speculations, our breasts rather than our inventions, for the great conservatories and magazines of our rights and privileges.

You might, if you pleased, have profited by our example, and have given to your recovered freedom a correspondent dignity. Your privileges, though discontinued, were not lost to memory. Your constitution, it is true, whilst you were out of possession, suffered waste and dilapidation, but you possessed in some parts the walls, and, in all, the foundations, of a noble and venerable castle. You might have repaired those walls; you might have built on those old foundations. Your constitution was suspended before it was perfected; but you had the elements of a constitution very nearly as good as could be wished. In your old states you possessed that variety of parts corresponding with the various descriptions of which your community was happily composed; you had all that combination, and all that opposition of interests, you had that action and counteraction, which, in the natural and in the political world, from the reciprocal struggle of discordant powers, draws out the harmony of the universe. These opposed and conflicting interests, which you considered as so great a blemish in your old and in our present constitution, interpose a salutary check to all precipitate resolutions. They render deliberation a matter not of choice, but of necessity; they make all change a subject of compromise, which naturally begets moderation; they produce *temperaments* preventing the sore evil of harsh, crude, unqualified reformations, and rendering all the headlong exertions of arbitrary power, in the few or in the many, for ever impracticable. Through that diversity of members and interests, general liberty had as many securities as there were separate views in the several orders; whilst by pressing down the whole by the weight of a real monarchy, the separate parts would have been prevented from warping, and starting from their allotted places.

#                    #

## PAINE: RIGHTS OF MAN[15]

Rights of Man, *Part I, includes a comparison between the British and French Constitutions. Paine also attacks Edmund Burke, particularly his concept of "traditional rights." In the following passage Paine argues that man acquired his rights at the moment of creation before the development of custom and tradition in society.*

γ          γ          γ

Before anything can be reasoned upon to a conclusion, certain facts, principles, or data, to reason from, must be established, admitted, or denied. Mr. Burke, with his usual outrage, abuses the Declaration of the Rights of Man, published by the National Assembly of France as the basis on which the constitution of France is built. This he calls "paltry and blurred sheets of paper about the rights of man"—Does Mr. Burke mean to deny that man has any rights? If he does, then he must mean that there are no such things as rights anywhere, and that he has none himself, for who is there in the world but man? But if Mr. Burke means to admit that man has rights, the question then will be: What are those rights, and how came man by them originally?

The error of those who reason by precedents drawn from antiquity, respecting the rights of man, is, that they do not go far enough into antiquity. They do not go the whole way. They stop in some of the intermediate stages of a hundred or a thousand years, and produce what was then done as a rule for the present day. This is no authority at all. If we travel still farther into antiquity, we shall find a direct contrary opinion and practice prevailing? and if antiquity is to be authority, a thousand such

[15] Thomas Paine, *The Rights of Man* (London, 1791), pp. 43-52.

authorities may be produced, successively contradicting each other; but if we proceed on, we shall at last come out right; we shall come to the time when man came from the hand of his Maker. What was he then? Man. Man was his high and only title, and a higher cannot be given him.—But of titles I shall speak hereafter.

If any generation of men ever possessed the right of dictating the mode by which the world should be governed for ever, it was the first generation that existed; and if that generation did not do it, no succeeding generation can show any authority for doing it, nor set any up. The illuminating and divine principle of the equal rights of man (for it has its origin from the Maker of man) relates, not only to the living individuals, but to generations of men succeeding each other. Every generation is equal in rights to the generations which preceeded it, by the same rule that every individual is born equal in rights with his contemporary.

Every history of the creation, and every traditionary account, whether from the lettered or unlettered world, however they may vary in their opinion or belief of certain particulars, all agree in establishing one point, the unity of man; by which I mean that man is all of one degree, and consequently that all men are born equal, and with equal and natural rights, in the same manner as if posterity had been continued by creation instead of generation, the latter being only the mode by which the former is carried forward; and consequently, every child born into the world must be considered as deriving its existence from God. The world is as new to him as it was to the first man that existed, and his natural right in it is of the same kind.

Hitherto we have spoken only (and that but in part) of the natural rights of man. We have not to consider the civil rights of man, and to show how the one originates out of the other. Man did not enter into society to become worse than he was before, nor to have less rights than he had before, but to have those rights better sec-cured. His natural rights are the foundation of all his civil rights. But in order to pursue this distinction with more precision, it will be necessary to mark the different quali-ties of natural and civil rights.

A few words will explain this. Natural rights are those which appertain to man in right of his existence. Of this kind are all the intellectual rights, or rights of the mind, and also all those rights of acting as an individual for his own comfort and happiness, which are not inurious to the natural rights of others. Civil rights are those which appertain to man in right of his being a member of so-ciety. Every civil right has for its foundation some natural right pre-existing in the individual, but to which his in-dividual power is not in all cases, sufficiently competent. Of this kind are all those which relate to security and pro-tection.

From this short review, it will be easy to distinguish between that class of natural rights which man retains after entering into society, and those which he throws into the common stock as a member of society.

The natural rights which he retains, are all those in which the power to execute is as perfect in the individual as the right itself. Among this class, as is before men-tioned, are all the intellectual rights, or rights of the mind, consequently, religion is one of those rights. The natural rights which are not retained, are all those in which, though the right is perfect in the individual, the power to execute them is defective. They answer not his purpose. A man, by natural right, has a right to judge in his own cause, and so far as the right of the mind is con-cerned, he never surrenders it. But what availeth it him to judge, if he has not power to redress? He therefore deposits this right in the common stock of society, and takes the arms of society, of which he is a part, in prefer-ence and in addition to his own. Society grants him nothing. Every man is a proprietor in society, and draws on the capital as a matter of right. . . .

#                    #

## HORRORS OF THE SLAVE TRADE[16]

*During the eighteenth century, some of the men who had worked on slave ships published an account of their experiences. The following is an excerpt from the memoirs of Alexander Falconbridge who served as ship's surgeon aboard an English slave trader.*

γ       γ       γ

The hardships and inconveniences suffered by the Negores during the passage, are scarcely to be enumerated or conceived. They are far more violently affected by the sea-sickness, than the Europeans, It frequently terminates in death, especially among the women. But the exclusion of the fresh air is among the most intolerable. For the purpose of admitting this needful refreshment, most of the ships in the slave trade are provided, between the decks, with five or six air-ports on each side of the ship, of about six inches in length, and four in breadth; in addition to which, some few ships, but not one in twenty, have what they denominate wind-sails. But whenever the sea is rough, and the rain heavy, it becomes necessary to shut these, and every other conveyance by which the air is admitted. The fresh air being excluded, the Negroes' rooms very soon grow intolerably hot. The confined air, rendered noxious by the effluvia exhaled from their bodies, and by being repeatedly breathed, soon produces fevers and fluxes, which generally carry off great numbers of them.

During the voyages I made, I was frequently a witness to the fatal effects of the exclusion of the fresh air. I will give one instance, as it serves to convey some idea, though a very faint one, of the sufferings of those unhappy beings whom we wantonly drag from their native

[16] Alexander Falconbridge, *An Account of the Slave Trade on the Coast of Africa* (London, 1788), pp. 30-32.

country, and doom to perpetual labor and captivity. Some wet and blowing weather having occasioned the port-holes to be shut, and the grating to be covered, fluxes and fevers among the Negroes ensured. While they were in this situation, my profession requiring it, I frequently went down among them, till at length their apartments became so extremely hot, as to be only sufferable for a very short time. But the excessive heat was not the only thing that rendered their situation intolerable. The deck, that is, the floor of their rooms, was so covered with the blood and mucus which had proceeded from them in consequence of the flux, that it resembled a slaughter-house. It is not in the power of the human imagination to picture to itself a situation more dreadful or disgusting. Numbers of the slaves having fainted, they were carried upon deck, where several of them died, and the rest were, with great difficulty, restored. It had nearly proved fatal to me also. The climate was too warm to admit the wearing of any clothing but a shirt, and that I had pulled off before I went down; not withstanding which, by only continuning among them for about a quarter of an hour, I was so overcome with the heat, stench, and foul air, that I had nearly fainted; and it was not without assistance, that I could get upon deck. The consequence was, that I soon fell sick of the same disorder, from which I did not recover for several months.

#                              #

# RANKIN: SLAVE'S RIGHT TO FREEDOM[17]

*A Presbyterian minister from Ohio, John Rankin, pub-lsihed* Letters on American Slavery *in 1833. In the follow-ing excerpt he argues for the humanity of the black man and his inherent right to freedom.*

γ  γ  γ

The Creator is infinitely wise, and consequently must have created every being in his universe for occupying some particular station in the scale of created existence. To suppose him to create without design, is to suppose him unwise. Again, if he has created every being to oc-cupy a particular station in the scale of existence, he must have adapted the nature of every being to the station for which it was intended. To create for a particular purpose, and not adapt the thing created to that purpose, would argue the greatest want of wisdom. Hence we conclude that if the Creator formed the Africans for slavery, he has suited their nature to the design of their creation, and that they are incapacitated for freedom. This would be accord-ing to the whole analogy of creation, in which every creature has a nature suited to the station for which it was intended. But we find that the Africans are rational crea-tures, are of the human species, possess all the original properties of human nature, and consequently are capaci-tated for freedom; and such capacity shows the design of their creation. It is most absurd to imagine that beings created with capacity for liberty were designed for bond-age. Did the capacity for freedom stand alone, it might itself be considered an argument sufficient to establish our point: but it stands not alone; it combines with it all the

[17] John Rankin, *Letters on American Slavery* (Newburyport, 1836), Letter II, pp. 14-19.

original properties of human nature; with it all these unite as so many heralds sent by the Almighty to declare that man never was formed for involuntary slavery. Every man, who possesses all the original properties of humanity, desires to obtain knowledge, wealth, reputation, liberty, and a vast variety of other objects which are necessary to complete his happiness. Now who does not see how inconsistent slavery is the with acquirement and enjoyment of all these objects of desire, and how directly it is opposed to the happiness of man? It obstructs the natural channels in which all his passions were designed to flow, contracts the whole sphere of mental operation, and offers violence to the strongest propensities of his nature. Does he desire to enter the delightful paths of science, and store his mind with such knowledge as is caluclated to expand the noble powers of the soul, and raise man to the dignified station for which he was designed? This is forbidden; an indignant master frowns upon him, and drives him back into the shades of ignorance and hopeless toil. Does he wish to acquire such property as may be necessary to render him comfortable in his passage through life? Even this is denied him; he is doomed to labor all his days in heaping up treasure for another; and to death, fraught with terrors as it is, he must look for deliverance, and to the gloomy grave he must go as has only asylum from his sufferings and toils. Does he incline to move in the honorable and useful spheres of civil society? It is considered a crime for him to aspire above the rank of the grovelling beast: he must content himself with being bought and sold, and driven in chains from State to State, as a capricious avarice may dictate. Does he desire to enter the conjugal state, and partake of hymeneal enjoyment? The pleasure of any unfeeling master may forbid the object of his choice, and cause him to languish beneath the torturing lash—her cries and her tears penetrate the inmost recesses of his heart, and seem ready to burst the tender fibres that twine around the seat of life; floods of tenderness roll from his eyes, but his sympathies cannot stay the cruel hand of the vengeful tyrant, nor heal the wounds inflicted by his malice. He dare not even attempt to console her grief by the language of tenderness, nor to wipe away her tears with the soft hand of compassion. I cannot conceive how flesh and blood can bear so much!. . . .

Finally, every man desires to be free, and his desire the Creator himself has implanted in the bosoms of all our race, and is certainly a conclusive proof that all were designed for freedom; else man was created for disappointment and misery. All the feelings of humanity are strongly opposed to being enslaved, and nothing but the strong arm of power can make man submit to the yoke of bondage. What, my brother, would be more distressing to you, than to have the yoke of slavery put upon your neck and that of your little daughter, that you might, with her, wear out your life in laboring for the wealth and ease of one who perhaps would not regard a single tender feeling of your nature? And though you think your slaves are in very comfortable circumstances, and I have no doubt but you treat them as kindly as is compatible with their present station, yet were you and your little daughter in the very same circumstances in which they are now placed, I think I would cheerfully part with all I possess to purchase your freedom, if nothing less would procure it; and if I should not, I apprehend you would think me an ungenerous and cruel brother. How then can you withhold from others what is so dear to yourself? The Africans possess all the original properties of humanity, and were, as we have fairly proven from their nature, created for freedom; and, therefore, to enslave them is both unjust and cruel.

#                    #

## DOUGLASS: LIFE OF A SLAVE[18]

*Frederick Douglass was born in February 1817, in Tuckahoe, Talbot County, Maryland. He was the son of an unkown white father and Harriet Bailey, a black slave. As a child, he suffered from considerable physical deprivation. In the following excerpt from his autobiography, he recalls the heavy work load of slaves and the cruelty of overseers.*

γ     γ     γ

There were no beds given the slaves, unless one coarse blanket be considered such, and none but the men and women had these. This, however, is not considered a very great privation. They find less difficulty from the want of beds, than from the want of time to sleep; for when their day's work in the field is done, the most of them having their washing, mending, and cooking to do, and having few or none of the ordinary facilities for doing either of these, very many of their sleeping hours are consumed in preparing for the field the coming day; and when this is done, old and young, male and female, married and single, drop down side by side, on one common bed,—the cold, damp floor,—each covering himself or herself with their miserable blankets; and there they sleep till they are summoned to the field by the driver's horn. At the sound of this, all must rise, and be off to the field. There must be no halting; every one must be at his or her post; and woe betides them who hear not this morning summons to the field; for if they are not awakened by the sense of hearing, they are by the sense of feeling: no age nor sex finds any favor. Mr. Severe, the overseer, used to stand by the door of the quarter, armed with a large hickory stick and heavy cowskin, ready to whip any one who was so unfortunate

[18] Frederick Douglass, *Narrative of the Life of Frederick Douglass* (Boston, 1846), pp. 32-34.

as not to hear, or, from any other cause, was prevented from being ready to start for the field at the sound of the horn.

Mr. Severe was rightly named: he was a cruel man. I have seen him whip a women, causing the blood to run half an hour at the time; and this, too, in the midst of her crying children, pleading for their mother's release. He seemed to take pleasure in manifesting his fiendish barbarity. Added to his cruelty, he was a profane swearer. It was enough to chill the blood and stiffen the hair of an ordinary man to hear him talk. Scarce a sentence escaped him but that was commenced or concluded by some horrid oath. The field was the place to witness cruelty and profanity. His presence made it both the field of blood and blasphemy. From the rising till the going down of the sun, he was cursing, raving, cutting, and slashing among the slaves of the field, in the most frightful manner. His career was short. He died very soon after I went to Colonel Lloyd's; and he died as he lived, uttering, with his dying groans, bitter curses and horrid oaths. His death was regarded by the slaves as the result of a merciful providence.

\#                    \#

# THE CIVIL WAR AMENDMENTS TO THE CONSTITUTION[19]

*These amendments ended slavery in the United States and extended the protection of the Constitution to the Negro. The Thirteenth Amendment was adopted on December 18, 1865, the Fourteenth on July 28, 1868, and the Fifteenth on March 30, 1870.*

γ        γ        γ

*Thirteenth Amendment*

Section 1. Neither slavery nor involuntary servitude, except as a punishment for crime whereof the party shall have been duly convicted, shall exist within the United States, or any place subject to their jurisdiction.

Section 2. Congress shall have power to enforce this article by appropriate legislation.

*Fourteenth Amendment*

Section 1. No State shall make or enforce any law which shall abridge the privileges or immunities of citizens of the United States; nor shall any State, deprive any person of life, liberty, or property, without due process of law, nor deny to any person within its jurisdiction the equal protection of the laws.

Section 2. Representatives shall be apportioned among the several States according to their respective numbers, counting the whole number of persons in each State, excluding Indians not taxed. But when the right to vote at any election . . . is denied to any of the male inhabitants of such State, . . . the basis of representation therein shall be reduced in the proportion which the number of such male citizens shall bear to the whole number of male citizens twenty-one years of age in such State. . .

[19] The official text.

### The Fifteenth Amendment

Section 1. The right of citizens of the United States to vote shall not be denied or abridged by the United States or by any State on account of race, color, or previous condition of servitude.

Section 2. The Congress shall have power to enforce this article by appropriate legislation.

#                    #

## THE PEOPLE'S CHARTER[20]

*The Charter which was presented to Parliament on several occasions represents a good example of the civil rights demands of the lower classes in the nineteenth century. All of its points eventually became law except the demand for annual parliaments.*

γ       γ       γ

### Equal Representation

That the United Kingdom be divided into 200 electoral districts; dividing, as nearly as possible, an equal number of inhabitants; and that each district do send a representative to Parliament.

### Universal Suffrage

That every person producing proof of his being 21 years of age, to the clerk of the parish in which he has resided six months, shall be entitled to have his name registered as a voter. That the time for registering in each year be from the 1st of January to the 1st of March.

### Annual Parliaments

That a general election do take place on the 24th of June in each year, and that each vacancy be filled up a fortnight after it occurs. That the hours for voting be from six o'clock in the morning till six o'clock in the evening.

### No Property Qualifications

That there shall be no property qualification for members; but on a requisition, signed by 200 voters, in favour of any candidate being presented to the clerk of the parish in which they reside, such candidate shall be put

[20]William Lovett, *Life and Struggles of William Lovett* (New York, 1920), II, 456-457.

in nomination. And the list of all the candidates nominated throughout the district shall be stuck on the church door in every parish, to enable voters to judge of their qualification.

## Vote by Ballot

That each voter must vote in the parish in which he resides. That each parish provide as many balloting boxes as there are candidates proposed in the district; and that a temporary place be fitted up in each parish church for the purpose of *secret voting*. And, on the day of election, as each voter passes orderly on to the ballot, he shall have given to him, by the officer in attendance, a balloting ball, which he shall drop into the box of his favourite candidate. At the close of the day the votes shall be counted, by the proper officers, and the numbers stuck on the church doors. The following day the clerk of the district and two examiners shall collect the votes of all the parishes throughout the district, and cause the name of the successful candidate to be posted in every parish of the district.

## Sittings and Payments to Members

That the members do take their seats in Parliament on the first Monday in October next after their election, and continue their sittings every day (Sundays excepted) till the business of the sitting is terminated, but not later than the 1st of September. They shall meet every day (during the Session) for business at 10 o'clock in the morning, and adjourn at 4. And every member shall be paid quarterly out of the public treasury £400 a year. That all electoral officers shall be elected by universal suffrage.

#               #

## WOLLSTONECRAFT: LIBERATION OF WOMEN[21]

*Mary Wollstonecraft (1759-1797) had ideas about female emancipation which were almost two centuries ahead of their time. She advocated a fundamental restructur of society which would make women the equal of men in every area of life. In the following excerpt she argues that women should be treated as human since they had the same God-given power of reason as men.*

γ       γ       γ

It is time to effect a revolution in female manners— time to restore to them their lost dignity—and make them, as a part of the human species, labour by reforming themselves to reform the world. It is time to separate unchangeable morals from local manners. If men be demi-gods—why let us serve them ! And if the dignity of the female soul be as disputable as that of animals—if their reason does not afford sufficient light to direct their conduct whilst unerring instinct is denied—they are surely of all creatures the most miserable ! and, bent beneath the iron hand of destiny, must submit to be a *fair defect* in creation. But to justify the ways of Providence respecting them, by pointing out some irrefragable reason for thus making such a large portion of mankind accountable and not accountable, would puzzle the subtilest casuist.

\#       \#

[21] Mary Wollstonecraft, *A Vindication of the Rights of Women* (London, 1792), p. 84.

## MILL: SUBJECTION OF WOMEN[22]

*The philosopher and writer John Stuart Mill was one of the most prominent advocates of feminism in the nineteenth century. In 1866, he presented to parliament the first petition for women's suffrage. In* The Subjection of Women, *Mill argued that "The power of earning is essential to the dignity of women." In the following excerpt Mill argues that the admission of women to all professions is in the general interest of society.*

γ      γ      γ

On the other point which is involved in the just equality of women, their admissibility to all the functions and occupations hitherto retained as the monopoly of the stronger sex, I should anticipate no difficulty in convincing any one who has gone with me on the subject of the equality of women in the family. . . .

. . . Is there so great a superfluity of men fit for high duties, that society can afford to reject the service of any competent person? Are we so certain of always finding a man made to our hands for any duty or function of social importance which falls vacant, that we lose nothing by putting a ban upon one-half of mankind, refusing beforehand to make their faculties available, however distinguished they may be? And even if we could do without them, would it be consistent with justice to refuse to them their fair share of honour and distinction, or to deny to them the equal moral right of all human beings to choose their occupation (short of injury to others) according to their own preferences, at their own risk? Nor is the injustice confined to them: it is shared by those who share in a position to benefit by their services.

[22] John Stuart Mill, *The Subjection of Women* (London, 1870), pp. 91, 94-95.

To ordain that any kind of persons shall not be physicians, or shall not be advocates, or shall not be members of parliament, is to injure not them only, but all who employ physicians or advocates, or elect members of parliament, and who are deprived of the stimulating effect of greater competition on the exertions of the competitors, as well as restricted to a narrower range of individual choice.

#                    #

## PREAMBLE OF CONSTITUTION OF THE KNIGHTS OF LABOR[23]

*The Noble Order of the Knights of Labor developed out of a society of garment cutters organized in Philadelphia in 1869. The First General Assembly met in 1878 and drew up a constitution. Under Uriah Stephens and later Terence Powderly, the organization grew in power and strength until, by 1886, it numbered over 700,000. The Knights of Labor advocated the principles of industrial democracy. Its members included men and women, whites and blacks, skilled and unskilled laborers. Membership declined rapidly after 1886.*

*The following is an outline of the goals of the organization which is included in the preamble to the constitution.*

γ       γ       γ

I. To bring within the folds of organization every department of productive industry, making knowledge a standpoint for action, and industrial and moral worth, not wealth, the true standard of individual and national greatness.

II. To secure to the toilers a proper share of the wealth that they create; more of the leisure that rightfully belongs to them; more societary advantages; more of the benefits, privileges, and emoluments of the world; in a word, all those rights and privileges necessary to make them capable of enjoying, appreciating, defending, and perpetuating the blessings of good government.

III. To arrive at the true condition of the producing masses in their education, moral, and financial condition, by demanding from the various governments the establishment of the bureaus of Labor Statistics.

[23]Terence Powderly, *Thirty Years of Labor 1859-1889* (Philadelphia, 1890), p. 243.

IV. The establishment of co-operative institutions, productive and distributive.

V. The reserving of the public lands—the heritage of the people—for the actual settler;—not another acre for railroads or speculators.

VI. The abrogation of all laws that do not bear equally upon capital and labor, the removal of unjust technicalities, delays, and discriminations in the administration of justice, and the adopting of measures providing for the health and safety of those engaged in mining, manufacturing, or building pursuits.

VII. The enactment of laws to compel chartered corporations to pay their employes weekly, in full, for labor performed during the preceding week, in the lawful money of the country.

VIII. The enactment of laws giving mechanics and laborers a first lien on their work for their full wages.

IX. The abolishment of the contract system on national, State, and municipal work.

X. The substitution of arbitration for strikes, whenever and wherever employers and employes are willing to meet on equitable grounds.

XI. The prohibition of the employment of children in workshops, mines, and factories before attaining their fourteenth year.

XII. To abolish the system of letting out by contarct the labor of convicts in our prisons and reformatory institutions.

XIII. To secure for both sexes equal pay for equal work.

XIV. The reduction of the hours of labor to eight per day, so that the laborers may have more time for social enjoyment and intellectual improvement, and be enabled to reap the advantages conferred by the laborsaving machinery which their brains have created.

XV. To prevail upon governments to establish a purely national circulating medium, based upon the faith and resources of the nation, and issued directly to the people, without the intervention of any system of banking corporations, which money shall be a legal tender in payment of all debts, public or private.

#                    #

# MUSSOLINI: DENIAL OF INDIVIDUAL RIGHTS[24]

*After seizing power in Italy in 1922, Benito Mussolini gradually created a state apparatus which the Fascist hoped would encompass every aspect of human existence. In the following passages, Mussolini asserts his collectivist view that man does not exist as an individual but has his real life as a member of the state to which the rights of the individual are subordinate.*

γ        γ        γ

Fascism sees in the world not only those superficial, material aspects in which man appears as an individual, standing by himself, self-centered, subject to natural law which instinctively urges him toward a life of selfish momentary pleasure; it sees not only the individual but the nation and the country; individuals and generations bound together by a moral law, with common traditions and a mission which suppressing the instinct for life closed in a brief circle of pleasure, builds up a higher life, founded on duty, a life free from the limitations of time and space, in which the individual, by self-sacrifice, the renunciation of self-interest, by death itself, can achieve that purely spiritual existence in which his value as a man consists. . . .

In the Fascist conception of history, man is man only by virtue of the spiritual process to which he contributes as a member of the family, the social group, the nation, and in function of history to which all nations bring their contribution. Hence the great value of tradition in records, in language, in customs, in the rules of social life. Outside history man is a nonentity. Fascism is therefore opposed to all individualistic abstractions based on

[24]Benito Mussolini, *Fascims—Doctrine and Institutions* (Rome, Ardita, 1935), pp. 8-11. Trans. anonymous.

eighteenth-century materialism; and it is opposed to all Jacobinistic utopias and innovations. It does not believe in the possibility of "happiness" on earth as conceived by the economistic literature of the XVIIIth century, and it therefore rejects the teleological notion that at some future time the human family will secure a final settlement of all its difficulites. . . .

Anti-individualistic, the Fascist conception of life stresses the importance of the State and accepts the individual only in so far as his interests coincide with those of the State, which stands for the conscience and the universal will of man as a historic entity. It is opposed to classical liberalism which arose as a reaction to absolutism and exhausted its historical function when the State became the expression of the conscience and will of the people. Liberalism denied the State in the name of the individual; Fascism reasserts the rights of the State as expressing the real essence of the individual. And if liberty is to be the attribute of living men and not of abstract dummies invented by individualistic liberalism, then Fascism stands for liberty, and for the only liberty worth having, the liberty of the State and of the individual within the State. The Fascist conception of the State is all-embracing; outside of it no human or spiritual values can exist, much less have value. Thus understood, Fascism, is totalitarian, and the Fascist State—a synthesis and a unit inclusive of all values—interprets, develops, and potentiates the whole life of a people.

#                    #

## WALLIS: THE FUEHRERPRINZIP IN NAZI GERMANY[25]

*At the Nuremberg Trials on November 22, 1945, Major Frank Wallis, assistant trial counsel for the United States, gave the following definition of the* Fuehrerprinzip.

γ        γ        γ

"Under the Commandments of the National Socialists: The *Führer* is always right. . . ."

Also, there are no legal or political limits to the authority of the *Führer*. Whatever authority is wielded by others is derived from the authority of the *Führer*. Moreover, within the sphere of jurisdiction allotted to him, each appointee of the *Führer* manipulates his power in equally unrestricted fashion, subordinate only to the command of those above him. Each appointee owes unconditional obedience to the *Führer* and to the superior Party leaders in the hierarchy.

Each Political Leader was sworn in yearly. According to the Party manual, which will be introduced in evidence, the wording of the oath was as follows:

"I pledge eternal allegiance to Adolf Hitler. I pledge unconditional obedience to him and the *Führer* appointed by him."

The Party manual also provides that:

"The Political Leader is inseparably tied to the ideology and the organization of the NSDAP. His oath only ends with his death or with his expulsion from the National Socialist Community.

As the Defendant Hans Frank stated in one of his publications.

"Leadership principle in the administration means:

"Always to replace decision by majority, by decision on the part of a specific person with clear

[25] *Trial of Major War Criminals before the International Military Tribunal* (New York, 1947), vol. II, pp. 182-183.

jurisdiction and with sole responsibility to those above, and to entrust to his authority the realization of the decision to those below."

The authority of the *Fürher,* his appointees, and through them, of the Party as a whole, extends into all spheres of public and private life.

The Party dominates the State.

The Party dominates the Armed Forces.

The Party dominates all individuals within the State.

The Party eliminates all institutions, groups, and individuals unwilling to accept the leadership of its *Führer.*

As the Party manual states:

"Only those organizations can lay claim to the institution of the leadership principle and to the National Socialist meaning of the State and people in the National Socialist meaning of the term, which . . . have been integrated into, supervised and formed by the Party and which, in the future, will continue to do so."

The manual goes on to state:

"All others which conduct an organizational life of their own are to be rejected as outsiders and will either have to adjust themselves or disappear from public life."

#                    #

## THE GENOCIDE CONVENTION[26]

*On December 11, 1946, the United Nations General Assembly adopted Resolution 96 (I) which condemned genocide as a crime in international law, determining that all nations had an interest in punishing such cases. Two years later the text of the Convention was unanimously adopted by the General Assembly. However, many United Nations members including the United States have failed to ratify the Convention.*

γ       γ       γ

### ARTICLE I

The Contracting Parties confirm that genocide, whether committed in time of peace or in time of war, is a crime under international law which they undertake to prevent and to punish.

### ARTICLE II

In the present Convention, genocide means any of the following acts committed with intent to destroy, in whole or in part, a national, ethnical, racial or religious group, as such:

(*a*) Killing members of the group;

(*b*) Causing serious bodily or mental harm to members of the group;

(*c*) Deliberately inflicting on the group conditions of life calculated to bring about its physical destruction in whole or in part;

(*d*) Imposing measures intended to prevent births within the group;

(*e*) Forcibly transferring children of the group to another group.

[26] Courtesy of the United Nations.

## ARTICLE III

The following acts shall be punishable:

(*a*) Genocide;

(*b*) Conspiracy to commit genocide;

(*c*) Direct and public incitement to commit genocide;

(*d*) Attempt to commit genocide;

(*e*) Complicity in genocide.

## ARTICLE IV

Persons committing genocide or any of the other acts enumerated in article III shall be punished, whether they are constitutionally responsible rulers, public officials or private individuals.

\#          \#

## KHRUSHCHEV: CRIMES OF STALIN[27]

*At the Twentieth Congress of the Soviet Communist Party on February 24, 1956, the First Secretary of the Party Nikita Khrushchev delivered a secret speech in which he denounced many of Stalin's crimes. In June 1956, the United States State Department published a version of the speech which has never been repudiated by the Soviet government. Though Khrushchev used considerable Marxist verbiage in his speech, in the following excerpts he is surprisingly candid about Stalin's policy of mass murder against certain ethnic and political groups.*

γ      γ      γ

Stalin orginated the concept enemy of the people. This term automatically rendered it unnecessary that the ideological errors of man or men engaged in a controversy be proven: this term made possible the usage of the most cruel repression, violating all norms of revolutionary legality, against anyone who in any way disagreed with Stalin, against those who were only suspected of hostile intent and against those who had bad reputations. . . .

We must assert that in regard to those persons who in their time had opposed the party line, there were often no sufficiently serious reasons for their physical annihilation. The formula "enemy of the people" was specifically introduced for the purpose of physically annihilating such individuals. . . .

Arbitrary behavior by one person encouraged and permitted arbitariness in others. Mass arrests and deportations of many thousands of people, execution without trial and without normal investigation, created conditions of insecurity, fear and even desperation. . . .

[27]*The New York Times*, June 5, 1956.

. . . at the end of 1943, when there occurred a permanent breakthrough at the fronts of the great patriotic war benefitting the Soviet Union, a decision was taken and executed concerning the deportation of all the Karachai from the lands on which they lived. In the same period, at the end of December 1943, the same lot befell the whole population of the Kalmuk Autonomous Republic.

In March 1944, all the Chechen and Ingush peoples were deported and the Chechen-Ingush Autonomous Republic was liquidated. In April 1944 all Bulkars were deported to faraway places. . . .

#                    #

# HITLER: ENSLAVEMENT OF INFERIOR RACES[28]

*After his unsuccessful attempt to seize power in November 1923, Hitler was sent to prison where he wrote* Mein Kampf. *This work is full of hatred against Jews, Slavs, and other "inferior races." In the following passages, Hitler attempts to justify "Aryan" subjection of "inferior races."*

γ        γ        γ

Without the possibility of using inferior human beings, the Aryan would never have been able to take his first steps toward his future culture; just as without the help of certain suitable animals which he knew how to tame he would not have arrived at a technology which is now gradually permitting him to do without these animals. . . .

Thus for the formation of higher cultures, the existence of inferior human types was one of the most essential preconditions, since they alone were able to compensate for the lack of technical equipment without which a high development is not conceivable. It is certain that the first human culture was based less on the tamed animal than on the use of inferior human beings. . . .

Hence it is no accident that the first cultures arose in places where the Aryan, in his encounters with inferior peoples, subjugated them and bent them to his will. They then became the first technical instrument in the service of a developing culture. . . .

All who are not of good race in this world are chaff.

\#        \#

[28]Adolf Hitler, *Mein Kampf* (Munich, 1928), pp. 287-289. Translation by the author.

## CARTER: AMERICAN SUPPORT OF HUMAN RIGHTS[29]

*On May 22, 1977, President Jimmy Carter gave the Commencement Address at the University of Notre Dame. He asserted his administration's commitment to human rights in American foreign policy.*

γ       γ       γ

. . .we have reaffirmed Amerca's commitment to human rights as a fundamental tenet of our foreign policy. In ancestry, religion, color, place of origin, and cultural background, we Americans are as diverse a nation as the world has ever seen. No common mystique of blood or soil unites us. What draws us together, perhaps more than anything else, is a belief in human freedom.

We want the world to know that our Nation stands for more than financial prosperity. This does not mean that we can conduct our foreign policy by rigid moral maxims. We live in a world that is imperfect and which will always be imperfect—a world that is complex and confused and which will always be complex and confused. .. .

. . .Throughout the world today, in free nations and in totalitarian countries as well, there is a preoccupation with the subject of human freedom, human rights. And I believe it is incumbent on us in this country to keep that discussion, that debate, that contention alive. No other country is as well-qualified as we to set an example. We have our own shortcomings and faults, and we should strive constantly and with courage to make sure that we are legitimately proud of what we have.

#       #

[29] *The New York Times,* May 23, 1977.

# THE HELSINKI AGREEMENT [30]

*The following is an extract from the Final Act of the Conference on Security and Co-operation in Europe which was held in Helsinki, Finland, on August 1, 1975. Unfortunately, no mechanism was set up which can compel the signatory states to "promote and encourage" human rights.*

γ        γ        γ

The participating States will respect human rights and fundamental freedoms, including the freedom of thought, conscience, religion or belief, for all without distinction as to race, sex, language or religion.

They will promote and encourage the effective exercise of civil, political, economic, social, cultural and other rights and freedoms all of which derive from the inherent dignity of the human person and are essential for his free and full development.

Within this framework the participating States will recognize and respect the freedom of the individual to profess and practice, alone or in community with others, religion or belief acting in accordance with the dictates of his own conscience.

The participating States on whose territory national minorities exist will respect the rights of persons belonging to such minorities to equality before the law, will afford them the full opportunity for the actual enjoyment of human rights and fundamental freedoms and will, in this manner, protect their legitimate interests in this sphere.

\#        \#

[30]*The New York Times.* August 2, 1975.

## DEMANDS OF POLISH WORKERS[31]

*The following is a list of some of the most important demands made by strikers in Gdansk as promulgated by the Interfactory Strike Committee on August 28, 1980.*

γ      γ      γ

Acceptance of free trade unions independent of the Communist Party and of enterprises in accordance with Convention No. 87 of the International Labor Organization concerning the right to form free trade unions, which was ratified by the government of Poland.

A guarantee of the right to strike and of the security of strikes and those aiding them.

Compliance with the constitutional guarantee of freedom of speech, the press and publication, including freedom for independent publishers and the availability of the mass media to representatives of all faiths.

A halt in repression of the individual because of personal conviction.

Guaranteed automatic increases in pay on the basis of increases in prices and the decline in real income.

A full supply of food products for the domestic market, with exports limited to surpluses.

The selection of management personnel on the basis of qualifications not party membership.

Privileges of the secret police, regular police and party apparatus are to be eliminated by equalizing family subsidies, abolishing special stores, etc.

Reduction in the age of retirement for women to 50 and for men to 55 or after 30 years of employment in Poland for women and 35 years for men, regardless of age.

[31] *The New York Times,* August 28, 1980.

Conformity of old-age pensions and annuities with what has actually been paid in.

Improvements in the working conditions of the health service to insure full medical care for workers.

Assurances of a reasonable number of places in day-care centers and kindergartens for the children of working mothers.

Paid materinity leave for three years.

A decrease in the waiting period for apartments.

A day of rest on Saturday. Workers in the brigade system [team operations] or round-the-clock jobs are to be compensated for the loss of free Saturdays with increased leave or other paid time off.

#                    #

## INTERNATIONAL COVENANT ON ECONOMIC, SOCIAL, AND CULTURAL RIGHTS[32]

*The Covenant on Economic, Social, and Cultural Rights outlines in greater detail some of the social and economic rights listed in the Universal Declaration of Human Rights of December 10, 1948. The following excerpts indicate its most important provisions.*

γ          γ          γ

The States Parties to the present Covenant recognise the right to work, which includes the right of everyone to the opportunity to gain his living by work which he freely chooses or accepts, and will take appropriate steps to safeguard this right.

The steps to be taken by a State Party to the present Covenant to achieve the full realisation of this right shall include technical and vocational guidance and training programmes, policies and techniques to achieve steady economic, social and cultural development and full and productive employment under conditions safeguarding fundamental political and economic freedoms to the individual.

The States Parties to the present Covenant recognise the right of everyone to the enjoyment of just and favourable conditions of work which ensure, in particular:

(*a*) Remuneration which provides all workers, as a minimum with:

(i) Fair wages and equal remuneration for work of equal value without distinction of any kind, in particular women being guaranteed conditions of work not inferior to those enjoyed by men, with equal pay for equal work;

[32] From the official text.

(ii) A decent living for themselves and their families in accordance with the provisions of the present Covenant;

(b) Safe and healthy working conditions;

(c) Equal opportunity for everyone to be promoted in his employment to an appropriate higher level, subject to no considerations other than those of seniority and competence;

(d) Rest, leisure and reasonable limitation of working hours and periodic holidays with pay, as well as remuneration for public holidays.

The States Parties to the present Covenant undertake to ensure:

(a) The right of everyone to form trade unions and join the trade union of his choice, subject only to the rules of the organisation concerned, for the promotion and protection of his economic and social interests. No restrictions may be placed on the exercise of this right other than those prescribed by law and which are necessary in a democratic society in the interests of national security or public order or for the protection of the rights and freedoms of others;

(b) The right of trade unions to establish national federations or confederations and the right of the latter to form or join international trade-union organisations;

(c) The right of trade unions to function freely subject to no limitations other than those prescribed by law and which are necessary in a democratic society in the interests of national security or public order or for the protection of the rights and freedoms of others;

(d) The right to strike provided that it is exercised in conformity with the laws of the particular country.

This article shall not prevent the imposition of lawful restrictions on the exercise of these rights by members of the armed forces or of the police or of the administration of the State.

Nothing in this article shall authorise States Parties to the International Labour Organisation Convention of

1948 concerning Freedom of Association and Protection of the Right to Organise to take legislative measures which would prejudice, or apply the law in such a manner as would prejudice, the guarantees provided for in that Convention.

The States Parties to the present Covenant recognise the right of everyone to social security, including social insurance.

The States Parties to the present Covenant recognise the right of everyone to an adequate standard of living for himself and his family, including adequate food, clothing and housing, and to the continuous improvement of living conditions. The States parties will take appropriate steps to ensure the realisation of this right, recognising to this effect the essential importance of international co-operation based on free consent.

The States Parties to the present Covenant, recognising the fundamental right of everyone to be free from hunger, shall take, individually and through international co-operation, the measures, including specific programmes, which are needed:

(*a*) To improve methods of production, conservation and distribution of food by making full use of technical and scientific knowledge, by disseminating knowledge of the principles of nutrition and by developing or reforming agrarian systems in such a way as to achieve the most efficient development and utilisation of natural resources;

(*b*) Taking into account the problems of both food-importing and food-exporting countries, to ensure an equitable distribution of world food supplies in relation to need.

#                #

# INTERNATIONAL COVENANT ON CIVIL AND POLITICAL RIGHTS[33]

*There is hope that the International Covenant on Civil and Political Rights could help to implement a mechanism for the rectification of human rights violations. An optional protocol provides that victims of human rights violations may petition the Secretary General for an investigation of their complaints. The following excerpts list human rights guarantees which all signatory states must provide their citizens.*

γ        γ        γ

Everyone has the right to liberty and security of person. No one shall be subjected to arbitrary arrest or detention. No one shall be deprived of his liberty except on such grounds and in accordance with such procedure as are established by law.

Anyone who is arrested shall be informed, at the time of arrest, of the reasons for his arrest and shall be promptly informed of any charges against him.

Anyone arrested or detained on a criminal charge shall be brought promptly before a judge or other officer authorised by law to exercise judicial power and shall be entitled to trial within a reasonable time or to release. It shall not be the general rule that persons awaiting trial shall be detained in custody, but release may be subject to guarantees to appear for trial, at any other stage of the judicial proceedings, and, should occasion arise, for execution of the judgement.

Anyone who is deprived of this liberty by arrest or detention shall be entitled to take proceedings before a court, in order that that court may decide without delay on the lawfulness of his detention and order his release if the detention is not lawful.

[33] From the official text.

Anyone who has been the victim of unlawful arrest or detention shall have an enforceable right to compensation.

All persons shall be equal before the courts and tribunals. In the determination of any criminal charge against him, or of his rights and obligations in a suit at law, everyone shall be entitled to a fair and public hearing by a competent, independent and impartial tribunal established by law. The Press and the public may be excluded from all or part of a trial for reasons of morals, public order *(ordre public)* or national security in a democratic society, or when the interest of the private lives of the parties so requires, or to the extent strictly necessary in the opinion of the court in special circumstances where publicity would prejudice the interests of justice; but any judgement rendered in a criminal case or in a suit at law shall be made public except where the interest of juvenile persons otherwise requires or the proceedings concern matrimonial disputes or the guardianship of children.

Everyone charged with a criminal offence shall have the right to be presumed innocent until proved guilty according to law.

In the determination of any criminal charge against him, everyone shall be entitled to the following minimum guarantees, in full equality:

(*a*)  To be informed promptly and in detail in a language which he understands of the nature and cause of the charge against him;

(*b*)  To have adequate time and facilities for the preparation of his defence and to communicate with counsel of his own choosing;

(*c*)  To be tried without undue delay;

(*d*)  To be tried in his presence, and to defend himself in person or through legal assistance of his own choosing; to be informed, if he does not have legal assistance, of this right; and to have legal assistance assigned to him, in any case where the interests of justice so require, and without payment by him in any such case if he does not have sufficient means to pay for it;

(e) To examine, or have examined, the witness against him and to obtain the attendance and examination of witnesses on his behalf under the same conditions as witnesses against him;

(f) To have the free assistance of an interpreter if he cannot understand or speak the language used in court;

(g) Not to be compelled to testify against himself or to confess guilt.

In the case of juvenile persons, the procedure shall be such as will take account of their age and the desirability of promoting their rehabilitation.

Everyone convicted of a crime shall have the right to his conviction and sentence being reviewed by a higher tribunal according to law.

When a person has by a final decision been convicted of a criminal offence and when subsequently his conviction has been reversed or he has been pardoned on the ground that a new or newly discovered fact shows conclusively that there has been a miscarriage of justice, the person who has suffered punishment as a result of such conviction shall be compensated according to law, unless it is proved that the non-disclosure of the unknown fact in time is wholly or partly attributable to him.

No one shall be liable to be tried or punished again for an offence for which he has already been finally convicted or acquitted in accordance with the law and penal procedure of each country.

Everyone shall have the right to hold opinions without interference.

Everyone shall have the right to freedom of expression; this right shall include freedom to seek, receive and impart information and ideas of all kinds, regardless of frontiers, either orally, in writing or in print, in the form of art, or through any other media of his choice.

The exercise of the rights provided for in paragraph 2 of this article carries with it special duties and responsibilities. It may therefore be subject to certain restrictions, but these shall only be such as are provided by law and are necessary:

(*a*) For respect of the rights or reputations of others;

(*b*) For the protection of national security or of public order *(ordre public)*, or of public health or morals.

Everyone shall have the right to freedom or thought, conscience and religion. This right shall include freedom to have or to adopt a religion or belief of his choice, and freedom, either individually or in community with others and in public or private, to manifest his religion or belief in worship, observance, practice and teaching.

No one shall be subject to coercion which would impair his freedom to have or to adopt a religion or belief of his choice.

Freedom to manifest one's religion or beliefs may be subject only to such limitations as are prescribed by law and are necessary to protect public safety, order, health, or morals or the fundamental rights and freedoms of others.

The States Parties to the present Covenant undertake to have respect for the liberty of parents and, when applicable, legal guardians to ensure the religious and moral education of their children in conformity with their own convictions.

#          #

## KENNEDY: FREEDOM FROM
## DISCRIMINATION[34]

*In his speech broadcast on nationwide television on the evening of June 11, 1963, President John F. Kennedy made it clear that at home and abroad the United States could no longer pay the price of racial discrimination. After outlining the confrontation that had taken place in Alabama that day over the registration of black students, the President made an impassioned plea for racial justice.*

γ        γ        γ

It ought to be possible, therefore, for American students of any color to attend any public institution they select without having to be backed up by troops. It ought to be possible for American consumers of any color to receive equal service in places of public accommodation, such as hotels and restaurants, and theatres and retail stores without being forced to resort to demonstrations in the street.

And it ought to be possible for American citizens of any color to register and to vote in a free election without interference or fear of reprisal. It ought to be possible, in short, for every American to enjoy the privileges of being American without regard to his race or his color.

In short, every American ought to have the right to be treated as he would wish to be treated, as one would wish his children to be treated. But this is not the case.

The Negro baby born in America today, regardless of the section of the state in which he is born, has about one-half as much change of completing a high school as a white baby, born in the same place, on the same day; one-third as much chance of completing college; one-third

[34] *The New York Times,* June 12, 1963.

as much a chance of becoming a professional man; twice as much chance of becoming unemployed; about one-seventh as much chance of earning ten thousand dollars a year; life expectancy which is seven years shorter and the prospects of earning only half as much.

This is not a sectional issue. Difficulties over segregation and discrimination exist in every city, in every state of the Union, producing in many cities a rising tide of discontent that threatens the public safety. Nor is this a partisan issue. In a time of domestic crisis, men of good will and generosity should be able to unite regardless of party or politics. This is not a legal or legislative issue alone. It is better to settle these matters in the courts than on the streets, and new laws are needed at every level. But law alone cannot make men see right.

We are confronted primarily with a moral issue. It is as old as the Scriptures and is as clear as the American Constitution. The heart of the question is whether all Americans are to be afforded equal rights and equal opportunities; whether we are going to treat our fellow Americans as we want to be treated.

If an American, because his skin is dark, cannot eat lunch in a restaurant open to the public; if he cannot send his children to the best public school available; if he cannot vote for the public officials who represent him; if, in short, he cannot enjoy the full and free life which all of us want, then who among us would be content to have the color of his skin changed and stand in his place?

Who among us would then be content with the counsels of patience and delay? One hundred years of delay have passed since President Lincoln freed the slaves, yet their heirs, their grandsons, are not fully free. They are not yet freed from the bonds of injustice; they are not yet freed from social and economic oppression. And this nation, for all its hopes and all its boasts, will not be fully free until all its citizens are free.

We preach freedom around the world, and we mean it. And we cherish our freedom here at home, But are we to say to the world—and much more importantly to each other—that this is the land of the free, except for the Negroes; that we have no second-class citizens, except Negroes; that we have no class or caste system, no ghettos, no master race, except with respect to Negroes.

Now the time has come for this nation to fulfill its promise. The events in Brimingham and elsewhere have so increased the cries for equality that no city or state or legislative body can prudently choose to ignore them. The fires of frustration and discord are burning in every city, North and South. Where legal remedies are not at hand, redress is sought in the streets in demonstrations, parades and protests, which create tensions and threaten violence— and threaten lives.

We face, therefore, a moral crisis as a country and a people. It cannot be met by repressive police action. It canot be left to increased demonstrations in the streets. It cannot be quieted by token moves or talk. It is a time to act in the Congress, in your state and local legislative body, and, above all, in all of our daily lives.

It is not enough to pin the blame on others, to say this is a problem of one section of the country or another, or deplore the facts that we face. A great change is at hand, and our task, our obligation, is to make that revolution, that change peaceful and constructive for all. Those who do nothing are inviting shame as well as violence. Those who act boldly are recognizing right as well as reality. . . .

In this respect, I want to pay tribute to those citizens, North and South, who've been working in their communities to make life better for all. They are acting not out of a sense of legal duty but out of a sense of human decency. Like our soldiers and sailors in all parts of the world, they are meeting freedom's challenge on the firing line and I salute them for their honor—their courage.

My fellow Americans, this is a problem which faces us all, in every city of the North as well as the South. Today there are Negroes unemployed—two or three times as many as whites; there is inadequate education; Negroes are moving into the large cities, unable to find work, young people particularly are out of work; they are without hope, denied equal rights, denied the opportnity to eat at a restaurant or a lunch counter or go to a movie theatre, denied the right to a decent education, denied almost today the right to attend a state university even though qualified.

It seems to me that these are matters which concern us all—not merely Presidents, or congressmen, or governors, but every citizen of the United States. This is one country. It has become one country because all of us and all the people who came here had an equal chance to develop their talents.

We cannot say to ten per cent of the population that "you can't have the right. Your children can't have the chance to develop whatever talents they have; the only way that they're going to get their rights is to go in the street and demonstrate."

I think we owe them and we owe ourselves a better country than that. Therefore, I'm asking for your help in making it easier for us to move ahead and provide the kind of equality of treatment which we would want ourselves—to give a chance for every child to be educated to the limit of his talent.

As I've said before, not every child has an equal talent or an equal ability or equal motivation. But they should have the equal right to develop their talent and their ability and their motiviation to make something of themselves. We have a right to expect that the Negro community will be responsible, will uphold the law. But they have a right to expect the law will be fair, that the Constitution will be color blind, as Justice Harlan said at the turn of the century.

This is what we're talking about. This is a matter which concerns this country and what it stands for, and in meeting it I ask the support of all our citizens.

Thank you very much.

#                    #

## RIGHTS OF THE AMERICAN INDIAN[35]

*In February 1970, a group calling itself "Indians of All Tribes," who were in occupation of Alcatraz Island, issued a statement of their intentions. The following excerpts from this manifesto reveal the deep frustration which was felt by Indians of many tribes across the country.*

γ                γ                γ

Our anger at the many injustices forced upon us since the first white men landed on these sacred shores has been transformed into a hope that we be allowed the long suppressed right of all men to plan and to live their own lives in harmony and cooperation with all fellow creatures and with nature. We have learned that violence breeds only more violence and we therefore have carried on our occupation of Alcatraz in a peaceful manner, hoping that the government will act accordingly.

Be it known, however, that we are quite serious in our demand to be given ownership of this island in the name of Indians of All Tribes. We are here to stay, men, women, children. We feel that this request is but little to ask from a government which has systematically stolen our lands, destroyed a once beautiful landscape, killed off the creatures of nature, polluted air and water, ripped open the very bowels of our earth in senseless greed, and instituted a program to annihilate the many Indian tribes of this land by theft, suppression, prejudice, termination, and so-called relocation and assimilation.

We are a proud people! We are Indians! We have observed and rejected much of what so-called civilization offers. We are Indians! We will preserve our traditions and ways of life by educating our own children. We are Indians! We will join hands in a unity never before put into

[35] From *Congressional Record*, 91st Congress, 2nd Session.

practice. Our Earth Mother awaits our voices. We are Indians of All Tribes!!!

We came to Alcatraz because we were sick and tired of being pushed around, exploited, and degraded everywhere we turned in our own country. We selected Alcatraz for many reasons but most importantly, we came to Alcatraz because it is a place of our own. Somewhere that is geographically unfeasible for everybody to come and interfere with what we would like to do with our lives. We can beat our drums all night long if we want to and not be bothered or harassed by non-Indians and police. We can worship, we can sing, and we can make plans for our lives and the future of our Indian people and Alcatraz.

What we want to do in the long range view is to get some type of help for our people across the nation. We must look at the problem back on the reservation, where it all begins, with the Bureau of Indian Affairs. There's going to have to be some changes made within our own government structure. We often thought of ourselves as a sovereign nation within a nation, but throught the years, this has fallen apart, because the state has beaten us on jurisdiction rights on different reservations, and the termination of the Indian people is close in sight. We all can see those things that are coming on and we want to avoid having our life taken away from us. What few lands we do have left on the reservations, we want to keep. We have no government for our own people and we live under what is really a colonial system because we do not select the people who govern us, like the commissioner of Indian Affairs, who is appointed by the secretary of the interior, who is appointed by the President, and the superintendent on every reservation, who is appointed by the commissioner. We must somehow make up our own plan of government for ourselves and for our people, rather than have someone else decide or plan what is ahead for us. We must make up those plans and decisions for ourselves.

We feel that the island is the only bargaining power that we have with the federal government. It is the only way we have to get them to notice us or even want to deal with us. We are going to maintain our occupation, until the island which is rightfully ours is formally granted to us. Otherwise, they will forget us, the way they always have, but we will not be forgotten.

#      #

## A PROGRAM FOR WOMEN'S RIGHTS[36]

*On July 11, 1971, the National Women's Political Caucus adopted a statement of purpose. Most of the reforms which it demanded were to become major issues in the succeeding decade.*

γ　　　　γ　　　　γ

The National Women's Political Caucus hopes to reach out to women across the country:

• To every woman whose abilitites have been wasted by the second-class, subservient, underpaid, or powerless positions to which female human beings are consigned.

• To every woman who sits at home with little control over her own life, much less the powerful institutions of this country, wondering if there isn't more to life than this.

• To every woman who must go on welfare because, even when she can get a job, she makes about half the money paid to a man for the same work.

• To every minority woman who has endured the stigma of being twice-different from the white male ruling class.

• To every woman who has experienced the ridicule or hostility reserved by this country—and often by its political leaders—for women who dare to express the hopes and ambitions that are natural to every human being.

We believe that women must take action to unite against sexism, racism, institutional violence and poverty. We will:

• Rally national and local support for the campaigns of women candidates—federal, state, and local—who

---

[36] Courtesy of Yoland Quitman of the National Women's Political Caucus.

declare themselves ready to fight for the rights and needs of women, and of all under-represented groups.

• Confront our own party structures, and, when necessary, cross party lines or work outside formal political parties in support of such women candidates.

• Train women to organize caucuses on a state and local level.

• Reform party structure to assure women of all ages, races and socio-economic groups equal voice in decision-making and selection of candidates at all levels—federal, state, county, and precinct.

• Register new women voters and encourage women to vote for women's priorities.

• Raise women's issues in every election and publicize the records on such issues of all male and female candidates, so that they shall be made to rise or fall on their position and action for human equality.

• Give active support only to those candidates for public or party office, whether male or female, who support women's issues and employ women in decision-making positions on their administrative and campaign staffs.

• Monitor the selection of delegates to the presidential nominating conventions for the purpose of challenging those delegations where the number and qualifications of the women delegates are unacceptable.

• Insist that there be no token female representation, that the women selected to give equal voice to women actually represent the views of women, and not merely to echo the unacceptable views of men.

• An adequate income for all Americans based on the determination of adequacy by the National Welfare Rights Organization.

• Comprehensive community-controlled programs for all Americans. They include: free comprehensive, parent-and-community-controlled child care programs, incorporating the highest standards of education, health and child development; free, comprehensive community-controlled programs for senior citizens.

- An immediate and concentrated effort to end discrimination against females and minorities in all educational institutions, public and private, including students, faculty and staff, with the immediate establishment of affirmative action programs to this end and public reports on present specific conditions.
- Fair treatment of working women—regardless of marital status—including full parental tax deductions for child care and household expenses; maternity benefits and voluntary parental leave for childbirth; change of the Social Security system to end discrimination against families with working women, and elimination of the economic and social degradation of women, whether by employers or by unions.
- Adaptation of institutions, public and private, to the changing work patterns brought about by the humanizing of both sex roles, with special attention to new solutions to problems of unpaid labor in the home.
- Support of federal and state funds for development of agencies at the executive level of states and territories to enforce equality and justice for women.
- Enactment of all the recommendations of the Presidential Task Force Report on Women's Rights and Responsibilities, many of which are noted above.

We recognize the economic burden of such sweeping social change, but we believe that this country's enormous resources could be more than enough. They need only be reordered to pay for life instead of for death.

#                    #

# BIBLIOGRAPHY

Bonnard, Andre, *Greek Civilization* (New York, 1957).

Brady, Terrence, and Evan Jones, *The Fight Against Slavery* (New York, 1975).

Brzezinski, Zbigniew, *The Permanent Purge—Politics in Soviet Totalitarianism* (Cambridge, Mass., 1962).

Buchheim, Hans, *Totalitarian Rule, Its Nature and Characteristics* (Middletown, Conn., 1968).

Bullock, Alan, *Hitler, a Study in Tyranny* (London, 1962).

Carter, Gwendolen M., and Patrick O'Meara, *Southern Africa: The Continuing Crisis* (Bloomington, Ind., 1979).

Chrimes, S.B., *English Constitutional History* (Oxford, 1953).

Conquest, Robert, *The Great Terror: Stalin's Purge of the Thirties* (New York, 1973).

Cranston, Maurice, *What are Human Rights?* (New York, 1973).

Deker, Nikolai, and Andrei Lebed (eds.), *Genocide in the USSR* (New York, 1958).

Dishman, Robert B., *Burke and Paine on Revolution and the Rights of Man* (New York, 1971).

Elegant, Robert S., *Mao's Great Revolution* (New York, 1971).

d'Entreves, A.P., *Natural Law* (London, 1972).

Friedrich, C.J., and Zbigniew Brzezinski, *Totalitarian Dictatorship and Autocracy* (Cambridge, Mass., 1956).

Genovese, Eugene D., *Roll, Jordan Roll: The World the Slaves Made* (New York, 1974).

Gipson, Lawrence H., *The Coming of the Revolution* (New York, 1962).

Gross, Beatrice, and Ronald Gross, *The Children's Rights Movement* (New York, 1977).

Gwyn, David, *Idi Amin: Death-Light of Africa* (Boston, 1977).

Hayes, Carlton J.H., *A Generation of Materialism 1871-1900* (New York, 1941).

Hull, Kent, *The Rights of Physically Handicapped People* (New York, 1979).

Kaufman, Walter, *Religion in Four Dimensions* (New York, 1976).

Kirkpatrick, Ivone, *Mussolini, A Study in Power* (London, 1964).

Kommers, Donald P., and Gilburt D. Loescher, *Human Rights and American Foreign Policy* (Notre Dame, Ind., 1979).

Lane, Ann J., *The Debate Over Slavery* (Chicago, 1971).

Lewis, Anthony, *Portrait of a Decade* (New York, 1964).

Lyons, David, *Rights* (Belmont, Calif., 1979).

Machan, Tibor R., *Human Rights and Human Liberties* (Chicago, 1975).

Maritan, Jacques, *The Rights of Man and Natural Law* (New York, 1943).

Melden, A.I., *Human Rights* (Belmont, Calif., 1970).

Moskowitz, Moses, *Human Rights and World Order* (New York, 1958).

Nielsen, Niels C., *The Crisis of Human Rights* (Nashville, Tenn., 1978).

Owen, David, *Human Rights* (New York, 1978).

Palmer, R.R., *The Age of the Democratic Revolution* (2 vols., Princeton, N.J., 1970).

Raphael, D.D., *Political Theory and the Rights of Man* (Bloomington, Ind., 1967).

Rostovtzeff, Michael I., *Rome* (New York, 1960).

Rowbotham, Shelia, *Women Resistance and Revolution* (New York, 1972).

Rude, George, *Revolutionary Europe 1783-1815* (New York, 1964).

Shotwell, James T., *The Long Way to Freedom* (New York, 1960).

Schwelb, Egon, *Human Rights and the International Community* (Chicago, 1964).

Solzhenitsyn, Aleksandr I., *The Gulag Archipelago* (New York, 1973).

Stanlis, Peter James, *Edmund Burke and the Natural Law* (Ann Arbor, Mich., 1958).

Strauss, Leo, *Natural Right and History* (Chicago, 1953).

Svitak, Ivan, *The Czechoslovak Experiment 1968-1969* (New York, 1971).

Wytwycky, Boldan, *The Other Holocaust* (Washington, D.C., 1980).

Yates, Gayle G., *What Women Want* (Cambridge, Mass., 1975).

# INDEX

# Date Due